RESCUING
FREEDOM
FROM A WOKE
CULTURE

 SO WHAT IMPRINT

MARK HAMILTON

Sowhat Imprint

Email: sowhatimprint@gmail.com

Website www.sowhat.ie

First published 2022.

British Library Cataloguing-in-Publication Data

A catalogue record for this book is available from the British Library.

ISBN 978-1-8382579-5-8

Printed and bound by:

W&G Baird Ltd, Greystone Press, Antrim BT41 2DU

'Love is wise, hatred is foolish'

Bertrand Russell

SOWHAT IMPRINT

SOWHAT Imprint reminds Western society of the existence of God and of why, individually and collectively, we need Him.

Available now from www.sowhat.ie

God exists – So What?

Belief in God is the most natural thing in the world. In this exciting and challenging book, the author demonstrates how we can be sure of God's existence.

'[A] great resource for anyone who wishes to investigate the rationality of theism, whether for personal or professional reasons... I would love to see all my students read this book – both for their own information and inspiration, but also as a source of ideas for teaching.'

The Gospels Are History – So What?

The inter-generational exchanges in this book reflect on the changing cultural landscape we live in while centring on the Gospels as being authentic historical sources in accessing the person and message of Jesus Christ.

'Wonderful introduction to the practical benefit of reading the true-life stories of Jesus Christ as accessed through the Gospels.'

Escaping the Bunker: Democracy Needs Christianity – So What?

The survival of democracy itself may depend on Christian commitment. Democracy needs to escape the bunker of pure or unenlightened reason and welcome again the light and heat of Christianity.

'It logically explores the political landscape and encouragingly points to a way forward to restore the damaged fabric of democracy on the basis of the Christian values on which it is founded.'

Our School is Catholic – So What?

Catholic schools have a great pedigree but are under threat from the wider secular culture. This book is a call to schools to commit to being truly Catholic and points the way forward.

'An important contribution to the debates of the value of Catholic education.'

For more information see **www.sowhat.ie**. All the above titles are available through the website shop. To get in touch email admin@sowhat.ie.

CONTENTS

MAKING SPACE FOR TRUTH

Millions died in concentration camps and in the killing fields of the 20th century for fundamental freedoms and beliefs that underpin today's democratic societies. A similar appreciation of freedom galvanised the Ukrainian *'On ne passe pas!'* response to the recent Russian invasion of their country. Yet in our modern Western world, these liberties appear to be lightly regarded, as evidenced by the steady implosion of support for the most fundamental freedom – freedom of expression.

Ironically at a time when runaway communication successes are tributes to modernity, a new suppressive tendency towards silencing has become part of the post-modern response. Now that we are technically empowered to say anything to anyone, anywhere, we have been disempowered from saying things that matter. Speaking our minds has somehow become a problem for us.

Information has consequences

The new world of freely flowing information has lifted a protective veil from all our institutions. Information that was once the purview of privileged knowledge-holders is now available to all, with this democratisation of information publicly exposing institutional fallibilities. We dare to call out and challenge the experts to explain themselves. We wish to know why news agencies report on some stories but not on others. We witness politics at work everywhere, shaping even medical truths, often operating under the guise of expertise. We raise questions about conflicts of interest. We seek transparency on public appointments. We want to know the detail as to why sanctions are not being imposed for international wrongdoing. Even warmongering itself, once solely the preserve of top leaders, is threatened as ordinary citizens wish to know exactly what their leaders have got them into.

Institutions and their leaders respond by using the defence of the schoolteacher of yesteryear – a reassertion of the same facts, and a call to respect authority. An inability to discern any institutional wrongdoing and a distinct lack of humility are often on show. Inevitably, such responses – if associated with untruths – eventually fail to impress.

But there also can be too much information sloshing around. Previously harmful – or harmless – gossip of poorly informed individuals, now turned influencers, can command the attention of the masses. Lone voices need no longer cry in the wilderness due to their capacity to garner huge online followings. Narrowly focused camera angles or crafted text with deep-fake intent, as well as unconventional political and philosophical outlooks, can make their way around the planet and into our minds via our pockets, or even into our children's bedrooms.

These purveyors of information may be John the Baptist figures or little Hitlers in disguise – who is qualified to say?

How should we respond?

This is where the elites and the experts come in. 'Listen to us', they cry, sometimes availing of the super-protective invisibility cloak of big tech, willingly proffered, to make potential unpleasantness go away. 'We will moderate content, impose order, curate the message.'

'Why should we listen to you?' respond many in the crowd, defiantly, buoyed up by their newly found knowledge, unconvinced by the credentials of the elites, yet wondering who they can trust.

And then, there are the watchmen, the big tech 'higher-ups'. With the help of self-appointed factcheckers emerging from a discredited – in some eyes, polluted – media pool, they decide who or what we should be allowed to hear and who should be silenced – for now or forever. Through information management these big tech players have the power to seek to shape whole governments, even in countries as populous as India, in their image and likeness.

We are constantly reminded that someone must take control before we drown in misinformation, or is it dis-information? There is now even malinformation, information based on fact, but adjudged by someone, somewhere as being inappropriately contextualised! There are potential putative big brothers everywhere – be they political, megalomaniacal, or commercial, all vying with each other for the privilege to exert control to protect us.

But take control of what? Real power lies in controlling the message, and so the battle is around that, whereas our true needs lie in reconfiguring the system's modus operandi and adapting the business model so that we are restored to the position of being a valued customer rather than being the product. All the while, the big-tech, wealth-generating, dynamic, positive feedback loops are driving us into factional tribal groups, precisely at a time when such tribal divisions serve unhealthy political ends. Difference in itself is not the problem; it is the algorithmic driven, deepening fragmentation that helps distance us all from truth, especially the truth about each other.

Controlling the message

Should the content of the message also be controlled? Do we really believe in free speech anymore, or are we glibly affirming so? If we do, why do we not even allow our comedians free rein? What does freedom of expression mean and why does it exist? This is where *Dare To Speak* enters the fray. Starting with questions on what freedom is, it moves on to explore what it means to be human and how we make our decisions. This naturally leads to an investigation of how we want to live together in our democratic societies.

Following on from the Sixties' cry for freedom, society expressed a preference for capitalism over communism and accepted licence as the meaning of liberty. Six decades on, those choices are being tested by unimagined (as of then) challenges: a globalised world, ubiquitous social media, big tech dominance, a viral pandemic, an impending climate change emergency, and a Western, self-created energy crisis that has upset the global world order. There are a lot of new zeros in the air: zero Covid, zero tolerance, zero carbon – enough to want people to zero out. Underpinning all that, following a long detour through the institutions, a divisive little brother of communism – known as woke culture – has emerged. The bitter fruits that are now vigorously sprouting up in our free societies are those of totalitarianism, intolerance and hate.

Will these fruits continue to ripen and be consumed by Gen Zers or can our present cries for freedom lead us to a better place? When seeking to assess the world's response to climate change, the UN Secretary General António Guterres reckoned that the world could be given 'an A in Technology and an F in Ethics'. *Dare To Speak* explores this deep fatal gap in our learning – which applies to much more than climate – showing how freedom, morality and conscience are all interlinked and why ethics (aka morality) has fallen so far behind in the development stakes.

Assessing woke

As the dialogue in *Dare To Speak* explores the paths of woke culture, assessing its rights and wrongs, and drawing on songs of freedom, it comes down on the side of the freedom of the committed over that of the wanderer. It proposes the Christian worldview as the one that best displays an understanding of the age-old dignity of humankind and its rules of engagement, while exposing secularism as the driver towards totalitarian outcomes. While some in Ireland may display an allergic response to the Christian worldview, this should not limit their acknowledgement that it was within the cultural freedom provided by Christianity that science, liberal democracy and even secularism itself found the free conceptual space in which to develop, the very freedoms that the secular woke culture is now keen to dismantle.

While in the US it may be making the most noise, woke culture is pervasive throughout the Western world, displacing the age-old left versus right political narrative with that of a progressive/elite versus conservative/populist divide. The ubiquity of terms like unconscious bias, white privilege, toxic masculinity, personal gender pronouns, self-censorship and taking the knee are indicators of its universality. Scientific research, financial investment, company structures, school pedagogy, college reading lists, commercial advertisements, Hollywood movies, college programmes, unanchored justice in Catholic institutions, and Diversity Inclusion and Equity mandates all testify to how woke thinking is taking over the civic culture.

According to its critics the danger of woke culture cannot be overestimated, not least because people under its spell deny its very existence – decrying the term itself as one that has been weaponised by 'the right' to devalue important issues. Even the language available to describe woke culture is uncertain – a term like wokeism still invites inverted commas. Woke is real, and has real effects, to the degree that it would appear to control the very ligaments of one's tongue. Political commentators who suggest that a 2022 election demise of Democrats in the US will sound woke's death knell are not acknowledging it for the cultural force that it has steadily become, nor appreciating the moral inadequacy of the materialist capitalist response to it. In the US whereas woke activism is primarily associated with Democrat politics, it pervades most agencies of government. Woke uses the guise of equity, which clothes itself in the wide appeal of equality and fairness, to totally empower a bureaucratic class to decide what can and cannot be allowed throughout society. In the woke world, competence and merit take second place to diversity issues, pushed along by governmental equity plans.

For its converts, woke is a form of enlightenment: once you see systemic oppression you cannot un-see it. A similar fate can befall its detractors and so the woke threat can be seen as ubiquitous. Yet the logic of woke is inescapable. In attacking all institutions and systems at their roots, all foundational principles remain vulnerable. Whereas searching for the right answers in Mathematics may, over time, continue to withstand any charge of white supremacy, a less exact science like Economics finds its principles are more amenable to challenge. Economics tell us that we just can't print money without some inflationary impact. Yet woke economists keep on doing so – as it 'feels' the just thing to do, post-pandemic. By the time economic principles are rediscovered, uncontrolled inflation and recession will have become embedded and will rule the roost for many years to come. It may also feel the right thing to do to have an open border policy with regard to migrants, but history (to which woke refuses to listen) tells us that all societies have real-world limits. The inexact science of climate change and the continual narrowing of the UN's IPCC window of opportunity to reduce greenhouse gases unfortunately provides a further ideal opportunity for woke manipulation and the generation of hysteria across western society, with arbitrary justice outcomes for all.

Is Ireland woke?

Ireland was a late arrival to the freedom revolution and often appeared a generation out of step with other western nations. The impact of information technology and the disproportionate presence of social media giants on its island shores has ensured that Ireland has now 'caught up' and has aligned itself with mainstream Western culture. The inclusion of Ireland among the woke elite was clearly in evidence in early 2022, in the days following a tragic murder of a young female teacher, when some of Ireland's NGOs' most political voices united with all mainstream media in a verbal war on Ireland's misogyny and toxic masculinity. That the murder was carried out by someone relatively new to Ireland and had happened in a country that has the lowest murder rate of women in the EU did nothing to temper the onslaught.

Surely this was an exercise in free speech, you say. Absolutely – it is great to be able to freely say what is on your mind – although, unfortunately, woke thinking does not agree that everyone should have that same freedom. The wokeness involved the overlaying of a tragedy with a new narrative, presenting individual facts of the case together with unfounded narrative claims, as if these were linked to the facts, as cause is to effect. This overwhelming, one-sided narrative, augmented by the woke silencing effect on opposing views, in turn disqualified others for speaking unless they were ready first to apologise on behalf of manhood. Not so much then an exercise in free speech but rather a partial, one-sided freedom afforded only to those echoing a woke message of misogyny.

There will be those who claim that the outpouring of anger was productive in drawing attention to domestic violence. This is undoubtedly true, and such hidden violence is an issue that deserves societal attention. But equally, we cannot ignore the destructive demonising that took place, which ensured the immediate silencing of many voices (who might have other views on masculinity or indeed better solutions to the problem at hand) and delivered an enormous blow to freedom of expression. One must ask what purpose was served by demonising all men for the action of the perpetrator? Who benefits from creating unwarranted fear and terror, making women fearful of walking the streets? Is it acceptable that woke culture can claim justification for heightening the awareness of violence against women while being allowed ignore all other negative outcomes of its actions?

Critics of woke culture claim that it promotes values-based conflict as its means of advancing society – it incongruously proposes that focussing on differences and on augmenting division is a path towards societal unity. It encourages self-hate and hatred of our past, rewriting history to serve those ends, and its method is one of divide and rule. It encourages the hatred of all those who will not join in in hating themselves and in hating the systemic badness of all that they support. On the other hand, woke defenders would argue that at least it challenges the gross inequalities and injustices in modern society, something that our existing democratic culture is abjectly failing to do. *Dare To Speak* explores these positive and negative appraisals, and how woke culture interacts with the freedoms that we all still claim to believe in.

Whatever the validity of some of woke culture's claims, its methods of silencing dissent have become deeply polarising influences on Western society. The only voices being heard are, on the one hand, those of progressive elites decrying the white nationalist reactionary diehards who wish to hang on to their institutionalised propaganda ('history'), and, on the other hand, those who are ready to face down woke contagion at all costs. Politics is not binary. Yet, the huge distance between these poles cannot be bridged if everyone else is condemned to silence; and without bridging mechanisms a common purpose cannot be found for society. In such a climate the real immediate problems of wealth redistribution, global warming, international migration, big tech dominance and world peace have no pathways along which to achieve resolution.

Although woke's cancel culture may truly aim to deliver social justice, it is an ideological dead-end. Cancel culture excludes and shuts down the oppressor, thus removing restraints on the oppressed. So, whereas the oppressed may benefit by being able to do as he or she wishes, it is purely an individualistic benefit, there is no societal improvement. On the other hand, social justice is only achievable through free speech and open dialogue around the levels of restraint society will accept – of which there must be some for there to be a society at all. Thus, cancel culture, while claiming to be a friend to social justice, is actually its enemy. Cancel culture is ultimately a nihilistic tool. Whereas freedom of expression within rational society will help divert society from marching over the cliff edge, the silencing of dissent makes such a disastrous outcome much more likely.

The tendency to silence others appears closely related to an allegiance to lies. State control of social media in China ensures that the truth heard is state-sponsored truth. The management of state media (and subsequent suppression of social media) in modern war-time Russia led ordinary Russians to believe they were fighting for the denazification of Ukraine. Yet, as our interlocutors in *Dare To Speak* point out, governments in advanced liberal democracies, working with a liberal media who consider that the end justifies the means, can also work hard to suppress uncomfortable truths. Numerous controversial examples are mentioned, including the Russia-gate hoax, the not-so-extremist intentions of Canadian truckers, the pre-election laptop story in the USA, and the origins of the coronavirus. It is highly likely that some readers, depending on their news sources and perhaps unfamiliar with *all* the factual evidence that has subsequently emerged, may still continue to believe these stories to be fake news or unproven conspiracies.

It may prove extremely difficult to identify what truth is, as evidenced by Wikipedia's own very long list of controversial topics where circular editing and re-editing takes place – Wikipedia itself being an initially neutral online resource which its founder, Larry Sanger, resigned from because of its leftist ideological bias and agenda-driven propaganda, partially due to it succumbing to 'mob rule' by woke social justice warriors. Yet, despite such difficulties, truth must remain as the overall goal.

Ultimately, *Dare To Speak* makes the case that our freedom needs to be actively rescued from the clutches of woke culture if persons are to experience freedom and if democratic society is to continue its forward march. *Dare To Speak* proposes that this can be brought about through a greater allegiance to truth, in this way creating a foundation on which trust, and thus the future for humanity, can be properly constructed. Woke culture is secular society's cry for deliverance from purposelessness; *Dare To Speak* shows that, for redemption to come about, secularism has no choice but to return and rediscover its discarded roots.

Historic, tell-tale signs of cultic influences on young captive minds include their denial of obvious everyday realities, and the exclusion of normal everyday influences from their lives. Modern woke culture thus stands indicted. Society is guilty of allowing itself to be willingly fooled. Young people who really do care for humankind and for the world they inhabit, would benefit from the woke 'exit counselling' that *Dare To Speak* provides for them. Ideas have consequences, including bad ideas, while ideas that are untested – due to the silencing of opposing voices – may produce the worst consequences of all.

THE SOUND OF SILENCE

Two friendly interlocutors dance their way to opening a long overdue dialogue with each other.

- Let's talk…

- You are being polite!

- Your sharp tone suggests you disapprove of my advance!

- Yes, that was my intention. Your request isn't welcome.

- But I think we need to talk…

- Need to? Do you know how judgemental that sounds? If a parent said that to a teenager, it would be harbinger of a major argument. Or if exchanged between a couple who were not getting on, it would suggest that it was show-down time.

- Yes, I accept saying 'We need to talk' has a disapproving ring to it, as if criticism is likely to follow. I am sorry about that.

- Apology accepted. But that does not make it any less judgmental in my eyes.

- How else then can I politely draw your attention to your non-engagement with me? I need to hear from you. As a basic principle of friendship you should wish to hear what I have to say. This is what conversing is all about. You know, listening to one another and exchanging views.

- There you go again. 'I should wish to hear what you have to say!' Should I? Really?

- This is becoming very difficult for me. I am fed up listening to the sound of silence. Here we are now caught up in Paul Simon's imaginary 'talking without speaking' of the Sixties era. We are close to each other but unable to communicate. I simply want to dialogue – to exchange ideas, share viewpoints. You know, to chat, to have a conversation, to talk with you. At this moment I can only echo Simon's refrain 'silence like a cancer grows!'

  You are mature, as am I. Why can't we talk, discuss… exchange views?

- I do that on Instagram all the time – you can see my views there. What you want to do is to sit in judgement on me, that is what I really think!

- It sounds as if your think it better that we do not speak at all.

- Yes. We can spend time with each other…and share things and continue to have banter. But not serious stuff, please! That way we can continue to be friends.

The moment passes. A week later, the verbal dance resumes.

- We need to talk!

- At least last week you were a little more polite! Now you are back to being your pushy self.

- I would take exception to that remark, except that I know you so well. Last week you told me that being polite made no difference, that you interpreted my request for a conversation as judgmentalism. As you saw no obvious value in politeness, I have dropped it on this occasion. We need to talk!

- There you go again! Making demands on me. Can you not leave me alone? Can we not be together as friends – without all this seriousness?

- Friends? What are friends if they can't talk to each other? That is what friends do. Do you consider what I might say to you so unbearable? You are very happy to do things with me, to waste and enjoy our time together, but not to have any real conversation. Why is that? Do I intimidate you? Do I scare you?

- Look, by asking these questions you're forcing yourself on me, trying to make me talk. I DON'T WANT TO TALK! How many times must I repeat that for you to get the message?

- Don't worry, I am getting the message LOUD AND CLEAR. You want me only on your own terms. In fact, it is not me you want, but rather you wish me to be a continuation or extension of you. I am good company and so am supplying a need for you, but I am no more than that to you.

You don't respect me. You look on me as you would on a captive slave, available to respond to your every whim. And might I add – to get full value for my money, since you have already accused me of being judgmental – your response sounds very tetchy indeed. What have I done to you to deserve this?

- Well, if I sound irritated, then let me say that your response sounds extremely rude. How dare you say that I don't respect you, that I don't have regard for you, after all the time that we have spent together and all the fun we have had? Of course I respect you!

We are now having a row over nothing, thanks to you!

- It is not quite over nothing. I do count for something, as do my views, although I can see now that you would prefer me to be an empty vessel. All I asked for was a conversation, and all you seem ready to provide is a full-scale row.

- There are a lot of accusations flying around now and I am feeling upset. I don't like getting angry. I am now deeply uncomfortable with where this discussion is going. Maybe we should talk about our relationship?

- Yes. That's a great idea. A conversation? Why didn't I think of that? Yes, we do need to talk.

- OK, but not now. I'm a bit worked up now and not in great form. Maybe another day?

Another week passes, and the tension further subsides.

- It would be great if you and I could have a chat, or as our old friend Paul Simon might say,

  Hello darkness, my old friend

  I've come to talk with you again….

- Sure, but not now. Life is very busy for me at present, and I have several college assignments to hand up soon. Most evenings this week are tied up.

- OK. I understand that. Life can be a treadmill at times – from work to sleep, etcetera…. It can be difficult to find time for conversation. But last week we did agree we would fit something in. I know I initially proposed it, but was it not you who then requested it of me?

- I am not sure there is much point in having a conversation. Can we not just leave it? You say you just want to chat, but is that your real intention? In any event I know what you are going to say to me.

- How do you know what I have to say, if I haven't said it yet? Are you prescient?

- Sometimes a person can just know things.

- Is that the real reason you don't want to talk to me? Is it that you think you know what I am going to say? Maybe you think I have said it all before to you? But then, why should that bother you? Friends often repeat themselves. Hasn't it always been the case that even lovers repeat the same sweet things time and again to their loved ones. There is nothing wrong in repetition per se, is there?

Surely, knowing what I am going to say can be a good thing – it could almost be reassuring? I don't understand how knowing what I will say should be grounds for not hearing me out.

- Well, I just feel that it will be a complete waste of your time and mine.

- What are you really afraid of?

- I am not afraid of anything! There you go, judging me again – suggesting now that I am fearful or cowardly.

I said we will chat, and we will, but not now. Give me some space. And time. 'Sometimes I get nervous when I see an open door...'

- That's fine. But please realise that all I am suggesting is that we have a conversation. I am not going to lecture you. Your supposed knowledge of what I am going to say should have nothing to do with it. And it won't be one-way traffic, as I also need to hear from you. This will be an exchange – if it happens. Friendships are built on such conversations. Go on and

Close your eyes

Clear your heart

Cut the cord...

- Yes, I will do that. For sure, our chat will happen! I may appear to be holding back, but I realise that we do need to talk. You are more persistent than many others might be, I will give you that. But I am taking that as a sign that I mean something to you, that you are concerned about me. That is a wonderful consideration – someone having my back and that I am not some unacknowledged, minor, dust-storm of particles drifting aimlessly through space.

People can achieve wonderful things when someone has their back. In acknowledging any great person's achievements, tribute is often paid to the partner who has supported them or indeed to the geniuses who have gone before, laying the foundations for them. In these days of uncertainty, with myriads of mental health problems out there, and with people feeling more alone than ever before, it's great to have support. Newton had the shoulders of giants available to him, whereas I have you. Thank you for your interest in me and for all your assistance. It really is much appreciated.

- I can see you are willing but not quite ready to talk, at least not for the present. Let's schedule our conversation for some time in the next week, then. By fixing a time we are less likely to let the opportunity continually drift and making it likely that it will happen. There is always a value in facing up to difficult situations, although I think we both agree now that this is not going to be difficult at all. It is going to be a simple, friendly exchange.

- Fine. Next week it is. By then, I will have assembled some of my ideas so that we can have a proper discussion.

- Assembled your ideas? But why would you do that? How do you know what it is I want us to talk about? Or do you now have an agenda?

- Well, it's sort of obvious at this stage. You want to talk about talking or, more precisely, about my not talking. We have not been engaging with one another for some time, except on a superficial level, and you want to address that.

TELL ME SOMETHING, BOY...

The logjam is broken and the reasons for the hesitation are discussed. The power of the modern culture to induce anxiety and to keep us all in line is intimated, giving rise to a promise of the future exploration of this theme... to move the discussion out of the shallows and into the deep.

- Well, I am delighted that, at last, we are going to have this conversation.

- We have only started and already I don't like the way you introduced that term: 'at last'. There is an implication in there that I have been avoiding this conversation or putting roadblocks in the way. I haven't! I have been busy; I have had a lot of college work and it has taken time for me to be convinced of the value of this discussion.

- I apologise if my expression of joy on being here has conveyed the wrong impression. 'At last' was not intended to signify any degree of exasperation or frustration, but was a sigh of relief that we both have been able to fit this conversation in.
  However, if I might venture to say, you continue to sound defensive, as if you have erected a self-protective shield around your-

self. Allow me to gender reconfigure that conversational duet from the romantic musical, *A Star is Born*:

Tell me somethin', boy

Are you happy in this modern world?

Or do you need more?

Is there somethin' else you're searchin' for?

All I want is for us to have a real two-way conversation. I have set no agenda, and I am presuming you don't have one either. But maybe these lyrics might prompt a direction for us in which to go. So, let us just talk.

- OK!

I confess to some degree of self-protectiveness. As you know I am a private sort of person, far from an exhibitionist, and I have some apprehensions as to where this conversation might lead. We live in an age where one's digital past can come back to haunt one years later, not to mention something said recently that might be repeated out of context. All my instincts are to avoid depth and to stick to the shallows.

- I think I understand you. Conversations can go anywhere. You may have to reveal something of yourself, and you may not be comfortable in that situation.

- Exactly!

- All that said, you know me very well. It is not as if I am a stranger or that you have volunteered to participate in some reveal-all talk-show. I certainly will not wheedle you into saying something you don't want to say. I suggest that behind your apprehensive-ness there is fear.

- We have only started and, already, I do not like where this is going. Are you accusing me of being afraid? Are you saying I am a coward?

- Absolutely not. I should unpack the word 'fear' for you. Fear is first and foremost a person's instinctive emotional response when faced with an immediate threat. Such responses are not some-thing you can initially control. So, if your response is an instinctive one then nobody can accuse you of being a coward.

A person can also experience fear in the face of *potential* threats or dangers. Thinking about a possible negative outcome alone, even one that may be very remote, can trigger the fear emotion. This is what is generally considered as anxiety.

- Anxiety, then, is word or a description I am willing to ac-cept. Ordinary lives of young people like me are lived in a sort of survival mode, with nervous systems slightly on edge, always calculating how safe circumstances are: fam-ily, health, relationships, finances. The result is, at best, an underlying uneasiness of where all 'this' is going. The same applies to my thoughts and ideas. Although, the beliefs and values of society surround and subsume me much like the physical environment of the city does, these are often not mine and can make me uneasy. The surrounding culture has educated me, it seems to have enormous invisible power over my emotions, yet its ways are truly not my ways.

So, I do confess to anxiety as to where this conversation may lead. In fact, even though we haven't really started, you al-ready have me confessing to some degree of powerlessness, acknowledging, as I am, that I am in the grip of an outside influence – be it benign or otherwise. I just wonder where all this is going to end up.

Is this going to be a case of my leaving the shallows? You know:

> I'm off the deep end, watch as I dive in
> I'll never meet the ground.

- I think it is. But let us take all this calmly. If you allow anxiety to invade this conversation, then truth may be the casualty. Let us agree first that emotions should be kept in their place, and that they are not to be allowed to dampen this exchange in any way.

- I am happy to agree to that, but I am not sure where the right place is for my emotions?

- Well, we may come back to emotions later. For now, we need them parked. I think we can lower the temperature by switching the focus away from your emotions and onto other less threatening ground, that is, onto how your culture educates you.

- That is certainly home territory for me. I am a creature of my culture, but I also a keen observer of it. I can talk all night about my Gen Z generation if we wish.

- That won't be necessary. But why not just explain what you mean by the invisible power of your culture and the anxiety it seems to induce?

- You seem to know more about emotions than I do, so maybe it is best that I stick to the topic of culture. One thing

30

that you don't need me to explain to you is how complex a creature I am, living in a complex world. My brain cannot process everything going on around me, so it takes short cuts all the time by making assumptions. I don't know how often when I'm out cycling that I find I am singing to myself, while my mind – which I think is on my singing – is making all sorts of practical background calculations and assumptions about traffic and pedestrians, without my being fully aware of what it is doing. Even while out walking, my brain makes hundreds of millions of calculations for every step I take, all usually unobserved by me. My vestibular system calculates distance, balance, the environment underfoot and even gravitational effects and only commands my attention if something appears not to be right.

Well, in a similar way, the culture I inhabit serves as an ever-present backdrop to my inner self as I move through life. It includes a range of value-laden presuppositions, with everything worked out as I travel along, all of which helps me to fit in. These presuppositions may all hang very well together or, as with my cycle journey, they may be a rather chaotic mix, but there they are, as if all ready-made for me. The backdrop is ultimately mine as I can decide what I wish to include. But insofar as I see the world much the same way as everyone else, this match up with others helps me feel at home.

- I can explain how your emotions fit into that picture for you. When you are in alignment with your culture, your emotions are usually well regulated. By helping to anchor you, your culture relieves, or at least reduces, your initial state of anxiety about the world and about those around you. I would add as an aside that if your culture is in any way discordant with the underlying reality of things that can become an additional secondary cause of anxiety, and much harder to identify as such, because we are inclined to accept at face value the backdrop our culture presents to us.

Now, is it fair then to conclude that your anxiety about having this conversation suggests that discussions like this are somewhat out of kilter with your culture? Is it that you feel more at home in 'the shallows', rather than the 'deep end'? After all, there is real trust between us, so it cannot be me personally who is the underlying cause of your anxiety?

I understand that you may feel that I might judge you, and that could contribute something to your anxiety. But is there something else, something in your social environment that is making the concept of this conversation an uncomfortable experience? Does your culture even approve of conversations?

- Well, I did say last week that I appreciated that you wished to talk about talking. And I accept that it took you some time to get me to sit down. That would certainly indicate anxiety on my part, which in turn might indicate that my culture is suggesting that I not talk with you.

And as I promised, I did reflect on this reluctance of mine. I am ready to share those considerations with you, to dive in at the deep end, but are you ready for a monologue from me?

- A monologue, although it means I have to shut up and listen, might be the best approach, as it will quell my habit of interrupting. That temptation is often too great for me – I find it hard to keep quiet. A monologue style will help you marshal your ideas and confront, in a non-pressurised way, any demons you might have. My view is that all your anxiety around this is partly a function of your culture. Gen Zers are more anxious than the generations that have gone before them, as witnessed by rocketing mental health problems and by the increasing number of trigger warnings everywhere. And they are also much more conformist – too much so for my liking.

- There you go, judging my generation again. So, not only are we anxious, but we are now conformist, whatever you mean by that?

- OK! I am sorry for reverting to type again. You have accepted that anxiety might be a feature. By saying you generation is conformist I mean that you are less willing to break ranks with the culture. Although you may think you are part of a rebellion against a corrupt system, you are actually following the script prescribed by the emergent Gen Z culture. This conformism follows on from the anxiety, in my opinion. If people are more anxious, then they are more likely to want to be part of the herd, to pass unnoticed. Or as 'gonzo journalist' Harold Thompson – who appreciated 'telling it like it is' – might have said about you: 'you are part of that generation of dancers, afraid to take one step out of line.'

What I am saying is, anxiety will make you more likely to conform and less likely to specifically rebel against any weaknesses in your culture.

- That is an interesting theory, I will admit you that. But for the present I have only confessed to anxiety about having conversations such as this. I don't think I have other wider anxieties, although I have many acquaintances who have, and no one seems to know why. Some studies indicate that urban air pollution can be a factor in mental health problems, others that there may be issues related to diet and air quality that impact on everybody.

But there are undoubtedly cultural factors involved that my culture does not want to admit to. I may keep my mouth closed, but that does not mean I am blind to what is happening. We pretend we live in an open society but much of our public thinking runs along a single track. Contrarian views would appear to be highly regulated by invisible cultural police. Society usually depends on media and academia to monitor and advance its development, but there is no guarantee that they will do their job properly. The greater freedom of recent decades has somehow been accompanied by a closing down of truly liberal minds. There are some questions that are never asked or addressed. For example, the psychological damage done to young people by the absence of fathers has been totally ignored for a generation because it does not fit some modern narrative that academia wishes to sell. I witness family breakdown introducing insecurity into the lives of many young people, these often believing that it is they themselves, and not their parents, who are the cause for the breakdown. This insecurity is widely ignored or denied by our society, as if to acknowledge it might somehow impinge on the personal freedoms of adults. But much worse these days is our culture's undermining of personal sexual identity, creating uncertainty for very young minds instead of providing them with the required security. When our modern cult of self is added to that mix of insecurity and uncertainty, then that becomes a very potent brew of self-doubt for young people.

Anyway, back to your challenge. On the next occasion I will deliver a monologue on how my culture approaches conversations and the exchanging of ideas. How does that sound?

- That sounds like we are making progress. That monologue approach will allow me to attend better to what you are saying, without you becoming sidetracked by imprudent interruptions. Nowadays, during even the most professional podcasts, the presenter can inadvertently re-direct the interviewee with an inappropriate or untimely comment. When someone has something worthwhile to say it deserves the full attention of the listener. I look forward to your critique.

- You may be surprised to hear this, but before we finish, I want to say that I am really very glad that we are having this conversation. Some of my friends – the male ones especially – just bottle things up. Sometimes it may be a mood thing, but it is as if they don't know how to communicate properly. On top of that, I know how oppressive our liberalism has become – our dismissive treatment and labelling of so-called vaccine doubters brought that home to me in recent times.

All that being said, I don't want to imply that silence is solely a cultural imposition. It can arise simply because men are very bad at listening to each other. There I am, ready to broach something profound, and my friend, as if almost sensing the unhidden depths ahead, moves the conversation onto the world-changing impact of last night's football match! Often, I am not much better than that myself:

> In all the good times,
>
> I find myself longing for change
>
> And in the bad times, I fear myself.

For most of us, our modern silence is a result of unwritten cultural taboos that I hope I can explain. If people feel that they can't honestly speak their minds with friends at work or when out together, what damage that must do to a society? I still don't fully understand why I was holding back but thinking through my thoughts should help clarify them, even for myself. I am already looking forward to another session soon.

- Well, I too am glad that, in my case, I persevered. But that is just the way I am. I try to hang in there.

I must say I am looking forward to you putting meat on the bones on how your culture converses. I look forward to your openness in addressing anything that might lie at the root of your society's reticence to speak freely. 'We are far from shallow now!' We are travelling this world together, so let us enjoy the journey.

FREEDOM HIGHWAY

A monologue on the failure of modern culture to understand freedom of expression, and how that failure results from a declining religious influence in society. The fruits of a jaded secularism – infused with the moral righteousness of an emerging woke culture – are addressed. Can freedom of expression ever return?

I must confess again that my reluctance to have this ongoing conversation with you has now completely dissipated. You may have thought that I did not fully trust you. Given how much I procrastinated, I cannot blame you for that.

As you proposed, I have reflected on my reluctance. The result is this report which is unlikely to make pleasant reading for fellow Gen Zers. But it is what it is. In any event, knowing that it is for your private consideration only and that you won't publicise it, I am happy to speak my mind.

Self-censoring

To begin, perhaps I should reassure you that I have never been 'cancelled'. I say this to be free of any charge of sour grapes that may be hurled in my direction. All my social media accounts are intact, unlike some so-called 'anti-vaxxers' that I know. It was not that these latter friends were against any vaccine, but their social media accounts suffered because they too frequently repeated their nervousness about receiving it. You might say that they came across to factcheckers as knowing too much! My virginal, pure social-media status has been hard won – I have good political antennae and I have kept all potentially controversial views to myself. In short, I have self-censored.

Freedom of expression has become disposable

I think it best to start by stating the conclusion of my deliberations and then show how I got there. In a nutshell, my culture has lost respect for freedom of expression as a fundamental principle and, in so doing, has lost its very understanding of freedom.

There, I have said it! It's out there now! I realise this is an enormous claim to make. I am also conscious that anything I say about the culture's weaknesses can viewed as deflecting from my personal responsibility for not speaking my mind. It is easy, others may say, to lay blame on the culture. And for clarity, when I say my culture, I speak here as a Gen Z person who has imbibed the norms, beliefs and attitudes of my age.

For the moment, I will seek solely to establish my first claim – that freedom of expression is no longer regarded as a fundamental principle. The corollary claim – that my culture has lost the understanding of what freedom is – will have to await your response to my first thesis. What I am saying is that whereas in all previous democratic eras freedom of expression was regarded as foundational, Gen Zers now regard it as disposable. Back in the early 1940s, a social justice anthem of Woodie Guthrie's caught the mood of the time. Originally leaning towards a communist worldview, the anthem, with some words adapted, was adopted in subsequent decades to reflect other interpretations, especially in the light of the experience of World War II. Since then, the song has become one of America's favourite folk songs, with hundreds of variations being recorded. Guthrie lyrics ran:

> This land is your land, and this land is my land
>
> From California to the New York island
>
> From the redwood forest to the Gulf Stream waters
>
> This land was made for you and me.

A universal dream like this is only realisable when we all can have our say. Once anyone is denied freedom of expression, then one can no longer voice a claim to 'this land', or any land, or any policy or law, or whatever meaning we may wish to give to the word 'land', not to mind having no further opportunity to pursue the claim.

Christian cultural roots are fading away

I like being definitional. Definitions are often good starting points – they can help clarify matters, especially when talking about topics as ephemeral as freedom and culture. Unfortunately, nowadays, even definitions are indirect casualties of society's lack of commitment to freedom of expression and the impulse to control how others think and speak. Rapid changes of meaning also have had a baneful influence on how we interpret the written past. Today, a word may be defined one way, and tomorrow (sometimes literally) if may have a different 'official' definition! As if anyone can ever truly plumb the depths of any word! Thus, rather than defining terms like racism or equity or freedom of expression, I will try to describe what I am talking about, in the hope that I can create a complete picture for you.

Let's start by looking at me. Who or what am I? What do I view as my culture?

First, I am a religious believer, a Catholic Christian. Some people might derogatorily describe me as an 'a la carte' Catholic or cafeteria Catholic. There is definite substance to those labels. I may not know a lot about Jesus Christ, and I may not imitate him as his early followers did, but I still see myself as a Christian.

The society I live in was once predominantly Christian – that is, it was one a place where Christian principles held sway. This is not to say that the society was ever anywhere near perfect, either by today's standards, or by the standards of those previous times. Like every society it had its many faults, as any right-thinking person should expect, looking at their own failings and realising that the 'Christian' world is not some idealistic utopia, but rather the sum total of the behaviours of all Christians, most of whom are like myself. I speak of this society as if it were now in the past, yet, when I look at my parents, at their lifestyle and their commitment to each other, I can still witness there the warm embers of that more Christian way.

But Christianity no longer underpins the culture in our society today. There are Christian elements to be seen – quite recently there was an almost comical employment tribunal report about a teacher and caretaker who had a tussle over the placement of a religious statue. But when it comes to the really important decisions, for example on life and death issues, it is quite difficult for anyone to publicly express a religiously inspired viewpoint without consequently suffering some identifiable public loss. Some of my friends are even afraid to have their pro-life volunteering links appear on their CVs in case this would harm their future employment prospects. It is not that Christian sentiment does not exist, but that when it shows its head, much like in a whack-a-mole game, it is immediately suppressed.

Secularism proposes living without God

This change has come about through secularism – a belief that religion is a completely private matter and should not be allowed to impinge on how the world is organised or how it does its business.

Secularism, which has evolved over two centuries into its present form, contends that God does not exist, or if he does, his existence has nothing to contribute to the way we live our lives. Without God, the important facts in the secularist's worldview are first, that the individual person exists, second, that the individual has a reason or intellect to navigate this world, and third, that the individual should seek to maximise his or her freedom to attain happiness.

Secularism has insulated itself from criticism by claiming as its own the successes of the market economy and of turbocharged scientific and technological advances. It points to our improved quality of life and to the modern successful separation of church and state. (It markedly fails to point to the true price of that success, including, for examples, the climate crisis, the waste crisis and the biodiversity crisis.)

These success claims provide more than enough cover for two obvious gaping holes in science-focussed secularist logic that might otherwise impact negatively on its dominance. It says that the individual is only a collection of accidental atoms, which through cosmic physical processes – and subsequently through biological evolution – has become the person that he or she is. This presents us with the first major problem – how can such a collection of cosmic dust be truly 'free'? The second issue that secularism cannot adequately address is similarly related to human origins. How can cosmic irrationality produce a rational mind? How is it that irrationality has accidently produced something that is the measure of it?

As far as I can see, the alternative logic – that God exists and has a plan for creation – fulfils the requirements of Occam's razor, that scientific rule that proposes, in layman's terms, that the simplest explanation is usually the best and most likely one.

Secularism nonetheless rules the culture with a claim that by society not taking sides on the question of God (and thus ignoring him) the playing field is levelled for everyone, whether they believe in God or not.

Secularism denies religion a voice

Whereas Christians show an openness towards sharing the public space with secularists, secularism does not display the same generous spirit. It seems to require that the religious worldview kow-tow to it, at least when it comes to the organising of our society. Religious voices must stay quiet, it says, on the rights and wrongs of things. By and large, religions have responded passively to that demand, partly due to an immoderate respect for the freedom of other voices, and partly due to the secularist hectoring and bullying that religious believers have had to endure in recent times. In any event, most of society seems to broadly accept the secular way of doing things – or using generally understood terminology – it accepts that no one 'should impose their morality' on anyone else. No matter how this is sliced and diced, when the term 'impose' is further extended to exclude even the simple expression of one's own views, then this phrase in itself becomes a byword for intolerance – indicating one fundamental way in my culture in which freedom of expression is denied. As long as one's view is part of the acceptable discourse, then it may be heard; otherwise, it must be silenced.

Some argue that this approach is acceptable because it is for the good of all in society. But when what is for the good of all is decided without including the religious worldview, then the very notion of good itself has no anchor.

Consider, for example, something that happens regularly in political life, that is, a proposal for the legalising of some progressive idea, that goes against a religious view of the world. A bill proposing assisted suicide could be considered as a clear example of that. Such a proposal will often be opposed, among others, by views informed by religious thought, claiming that the ending of life is not our decision to make. The majority – whether unduly influenced by a progressive-leaning media or swayed by emotional claims, or by what they see as the rights of the argument, or by simply following the lead of the secularist culture – may end up taking the side of the progressive view, seeing this as augmenting personal freedom. Then, not only does the progressive idea in due course become law but the secularist way seems to require that the alternative viewpoint be subsequently silenced.

That silencing is achieved in several different ways. First, a progressive media may employ bullying tactics to silence such 'religious' voices (and other non-religious voices which are conveniently deemed religious, thus providing grounds on which to silence them), both before and after the passing of the law. Second, progressive voices will continue to point at anyone continuing to espouse or support the 'religious' view, accusing them of not only rejecting the democratic will but also of seeking to 'impose' their viewpoint on freedom-loving people. Third, whatever is needed by way of compelling compliance, conformity or acceptance of the new law is employed. The notion of conscientious objection is seldom entertained. This may include the marginalisation of those who opposed, or continue to oppose, the new arrangements. Thus, in the name of greater freedom for some, the freedom of others to oppose is essentially eliminated.

Is this a good thing? The desired 'progress' may be achieved – but at the price of a possible pre-emptive silencing of the 'religious' voice, and the post-operative silencing of any voice that refuses to be cowed by the new thinking.

Such a secular society is not a level playing field. Nor is it behaving in an 'inclusive' manner. Nor can it be described as permitting true freedom of expression. However, in a secular democracy, once the majority principle is satisfied, then all else can be presented as being well.

A short step from secularism to a more moral wokeness

Over the past decade, secular society, under the influence of us Gen Zers, has moved a step further to become a woke secular one, wokeness being a further extension of secularist thought.

Secularism says there are no truths outside of those we make ourselves, and thus all our structures and institutions have been made and shaped by humanity. Wokeness brings an additional dimension to that. It says that in shaping our society in its beginnings, the negative influences of imperialist, white, male, straight oppressors held sway, and that this is the source of the systemic racism, colonialism, and sexism we witness today. Now is the time, wokeness argues, to overthrow all these structures and to begin again.

Wokeness, spawned out of secularism, does not consider itself religious. Nonetheless, it is driven by the engine of a morality – that of seeking justice and equality for all oppressed groups within society. It has crept up on a selfishly focused secularism that was starved of morality, and it has sandbagged it, now to become the new culture of the West.

The need for free expression

I feel this cultural background is necessary to explain how freedom of expression has become one of the casualties of my now woke culture. Freedom of expression has its foundations in our human nature, which the Christian worldview sees as being that of intellectual creatures created equal and made in the image and likeness of God. We have our individuality, but we are also highly interdependent, relying on each other in many differing ways. We must share this planet together for the foreseeable future, despite what Elon Musk's space missions might appear to promise us.

Our interdependence and our co-existent needs require that we be able to express our views clearly to each other, to talk and argue, to develop a shared story, to manage our social interactions. Through genuine openness we hammer out agreement, which – because it is freely entered – becomes more lasting. Freedom of expression, that freedom which allows us to converse liberally with each other, is a rock on which our society is therefore built. It is a necessity of co-existence.

Secularism initially inherited this notion of freedom of expression from the pre-existing Christian culture and accepted it, with adaptations. Whereas Christianity saw it as a principle of our nature, secularism understood it as a convenience. Once secularism had found a way within the parameters of freedom of expression to denigrate, devalue and finally silence the 'religious' voice, then it happily settled for the convenience. Secularism's continued support for many of the 'religious' foundational principles of democratic society which are now under threat – freedom of expression being a prime example – remains conditional on their convenience or utility value.

A convenience for secularism becomes an obstacle to woke

Whereas this old-fashioned secularism pretended to be a level playing field when it came to freedom of expression, wokeness shows no such piety towards any of society's foundational principles. In particular, wokeness displays no love for freedom of expression. It sees this freedom as part of those failed systemic roots of society. As one of those conveniences used by liberal society from the beginning, it is seen as having directly contributed to all the systemic injustices we witness today. Freedom of expression is seen as a primary method used by dominant oppressor narratives to drown out the discourses of the oppressed. It is a systemic weapon that has been used to silence the powerless.

Wokeness requires that oppressor narratives no longer be heard so that minority discourses can help bring about the changes that society needs. The only acceptable discourses are those supported by a narrow ideological woke viewpoint. Wokeness advocates using whatever weapons are available to it to silence the dominant discourse, abandoning all foundational principles of equal treatment or equal respect along the way.

This is achieved by not listening to the oppressor and by seeking protection from oppressor voices through requiring trigger warnings or demanding safe spaces. Or one can go a step further by censoring or denying any voice or platform to the existing dominant narrative. Taking it even further might mean ensuring that oppressor publications are removed from the public square, that oppressor-sponsored research be suppressed or that oppressors be denied access to employment in academia. In the USA today, over 70% of academic research funding requests fail the woke test and so do not get federal funding approval. In this new culture, there can be no universal freedom of expression. The platform of the oppressed class is the only one from which one can speak, and even then, that person can only express the pre-determined view of one's class. Anything else gets cancelled. Period.

Suppressing opposition voices is not new

This new understanding of who can and should speak in the public square seems a long way from where democracy began. Even to the un-sophisticated eye it looks more like the so-called 'freedoms' experienced under communism in Stalin's Russia, Mao's China, or Pol Pot's Cambodia, or in the Democratic Republic of Germany (aka East Germany). The old ugly is the new pretty. The suppression of alternative viewpoints is a trademark of totalitarian mindsets.

A friend once told me about his grandmother, a Chinese 'barefoot doctor', during Chairman Mao's cultural revolution. In a rural village, this then-young woman, infatuated with the revolution, treated a deaf mute who made some approving grunts as she carried out the acupuncture. She later told the village chief the astounding news that the man had spoken to her. What was it that he had said only, 'Long live Chairman Mao!' There was jubilation and celebration in the village that very evening due to the miraculous cure of the deaf mute – no one was prepared to contradict the doctor's unbelievable assertion. A similar silencing can be witnessed right across the West today.

It was not for nothing that Aleksandr Solzhenitsyn had to ingeniously hide away all his typescripts of Gulag memories from the Russian authorities before eventually being able to publish these for the world to read in 1973. These manuscripts, detailing countless personal stories, dramatically exposed the many lies underpinning communism. The enormous impact of their release on the world's view of communism revealed why, to the totalitarian mind, they had at all costs to be suppressed.

The air I must breathe

What has all that got to do with me? Why am I outlining this big picture? Well, this is the culture in which I live. My early sympathies lay with the Christian worldview of free expression, but I suspect now that my loyalties are mixed as I must navigate in tricky waters. The secular culture has pushed me along a politically correct road, where, adapting an old phrase for a new purpose, 'I must mind my P's and Q's'. This carefulness allows me to survive without public criticism. I have kept my religious views to myself for the same reason – but additionally, I have always been a private type of person. (Maybe I overstate the case when I say I have 'kept' my religious views, as by not being allowed to advertise them, I have also neglected them.) Now I have a new woke culture confronting me, one that has considerable strength, as judged by the enormous conformity among media and political elite.

Woke-inspired narratives are seldom publicly opposed except in occasional published newspaper 'letters to the editor'. The Irish Health Service Executive worked with media companies to secretly vet and achieve the suppression and removal of uncomfortable pandemic truths from social media posts. Champion contrarians such as Messrs Hook, Waters and Myers have long been banished from the Irish airwaves for their viewpoint misdemeanours, serving as an example and lesson to other broadcasters. Ireland's national broadcasting channel went a full year without producing any material or interviewes from a prolife perspective, a viewpoint that received support from a significant sector within society only two years previously. Facebook, aware that prolife voices had substantial advertising money to spend in the closing weeks of the 2018 Abortion Referendum, suddenly banned all advertising and successfully suppressed that voice. Irish politicians, on the left and on the right, conscious of woke power, now substantially agree on what one would normally expect to be contentious areas of social legislation, with their soundbites often interchangeable.

Suffocating with anxiety

What can I say? Have I really a right to say it? What will happen to me should I say it? I often consider that I must be alone in my viewpoints as no one else is saying what I think. But then, how can one know what others think if no one speaks? Can I really make this statement in that company – with this group of friends or work colleagues? These are all questions that trouble me on a regular basis. People often say that our generation are very honest – so why is it that I feel societal pressure to present a dishonest face to the world?

Does that sound like a bundle of anxiety? Well, that is what I have become. My primary sense of security comes from my alignment with the culture. I constantly feel that I striving to walk a straight line down the aisle of a fast-moving train. This pressure to conform creates deep unease within me.

Woke culture may be delighted, believing it is making progress and that justice and equality are around the corner as a result, but it doesn't feel delightful to me. For me there is neither freedom nor expression – just an anxious silence. I am hoping, like St Thomas More, that this will be enough for me to keep my head. A world that claims to have released so many people from closets has locked up even greater numbers of persons in the silence of their own minds, which at least they feel is a safe refuge!

So, when you invited me to have our conversation, I displayed a reluctance. I was anxious that you might ask me to speak my mind, and that what I said might go public. I had no idea then where the conversation might lead – how it might seek to pit me against the culture. Maybe now you can begin now to understand the source of my anxiety? The invisible hand of culture rests on my shoulder and, despite my misgivings, it is not easy for me to dislodge it.

Despite the good that woke may see itself achieving, if I am to walk that 'freedom highway' of Woodie's where 'nobody living can ever make me turn back' then I must first, at least, be entitled to voice my views. I look forward to enjoying the freedom of that day:

When the sun come shining, then I was strolling

And the wheat fields waving and the dust clouds rolling

The voice was chanting as the fog was lifting

This land was made for you and me.

This freedom was made for you and me.

TURN, TURN, TURN

Again, 'the times they are a-changin'. But on this occasion, it is under the cloak of a woke culture. The barriers to engagement with woke warriors are real and are hard to scale. Woke's exclusion of opposing voices from the public square may leave valuable answers 'blowin in the wind', creating an existential threat to democracy. An attempt to move the dialogue between our interlocutors back to the personal flounders on the charge of judgementalism.

- Thank you for that helpful explanation of your anxiety around talking. I was unaware that simply proposing a conversation to you could make you so unsettled. I persisted, and your good sense has led us to where we are now, on the road to mutual understanding. I don't think I bullied you into anything, but I was certainly tenacious. And, as you say, I may have displayed a judgmental tone. Perhaps that was a necessary provocation to gain your full attention and for you to take my conversations request seriously. However, I am glad you are not one of those woke warriors (as they are called) – I know of no way to break down their barriers to communication.

- Yes, my fully woke friends erect their barriers very high. I live in that culture but am somewhat insulated from it, perhaps because of my Christian roots, whereas many of my friends are all in, totally immersed in woke thinking. Safe spaces may sound like a joke to those who do not understand, but woke warriors need them – they are a necessary consequence of the societal dysfunctionality created by the impact of wokeness.

Some people believe that wokeness can be dismissed as a passing fad. I am not one of them. It has been fermenting in third-level colleges for the past forty years waiting for its time to arrive, so it is hardly going to disappear in the heat of the noon-day sun.

That time appears to be now. Institutional unwillingness to roundly criticise the many nonsense ideas associated with woke thinking is proof positive that woke-time is here. In fact, very large corporate institutions such as Amazon and Disney appear intent on embracing woke. To take one current example, woke thinking asks us to accept the conflation of sex and gender, and to acquiesce to the replacement of sex-segregated sports with gender-segregated sports. That this will destroy female participation in sports is obvious, so some workaround may eventually come about. This specific example testifies to the power of woke culture – despite the absurdity of genderised sports, some major international sporting organisations have easily succumbed to such woke demands.

'Turn, turn, turn' the protest song says, echoing one of the Old Testament *Wisdom* books, acknowledging that revolutions can happen within cultures, that societal change is a reality. Much like everything else in our modern society, the turning is happening at a very rapid pace. Nowadays NGOs, commercial companies and colleges nowadays are issuing so many solidarity statements aligning themselves with social justice activism that the public are suffering from statement fatigue! And there is no indication that we have reached anywhere near peak-woke.

Woke warriors are not free from their own suffering within this fast-evolving society. They have been educated to be hyper alert to injustice and are thus in a perpetual state of anxiety, which is augmented when their demands don't lead to instant action or change. With injustice everywhere it is easy to become worn out. Even things that are part of everyday ordinariness, for example speaking of pregnant women instead of pregnant people, can be a trigger for woke people. For truly woke people there can be no joy, only sadness and suffering, as injustice is a constant in our world – thus they have no resources to sustain themselves, other than sheer willpower.

One approaches a fully woke person at one own's peril, especially if one is from any of the designated oppressor classes – white? male? straight? coloniser? all the aforementioned? Some warriors live as if they exist in the centre of a minefield – all approaches to them likely ending in an explosive disaster.

Despite all that, there is a map through those minefields, for those who have the patience to use it. It could have as its title 'TRUST'. The ancient human basis for effective communication has always been trust. It opens doors between persons. A neighbour who voluntarily cuts one's lawn or takes in their FedEx parcel delivery, while seeking nothing in return, is perhaps one whom a woke warrior might begin to trust. If I forget about your rudeness for a moment, then this method of building trust vaguely mirrors the approach you used with me – step by step you scaled the (admittedly low) defences against anxiety that I had constructed around myself.

- That is valuable wisdom. One-on-one honest engagement has always been the way to make progress. Moving from the personal to the political, rather than the other way around, is certainly the way to get through to people.

Given that we are now being honest with each other and happily trading insults, I feel emboldened now to suggest that what you have explained to me as your anxiety sounds more like cowardice. Anxiety, as we have discussed, is a natural emotion – a spontaneous response. The Covid pandemic and the heightened fears about the virus has been a major source of anxiety for many people, despite the vaccines. But once anxiety is experienced, a person is meant to evaluate the source of the anxiety and appraise its credibility. With your own level of woke scepticism, added to your Christian understanding of the world, you should have been well positioned to see that your anxiety was misplaced. A braver person would then move beyond anxiety, whereas it is a coward who lets it hold him back. You have lacked courage!

- There you go again. Moralising, and judging me again. Telling me what is right and wrong, good versus bad. Now it is bravery versus cowardice.

- I am afraid it is a habit I frequently fall into. Again, I should apologise. You are right. I should stick with the facts of the matter and leave all judgements to one side. Let's continue to work with what we are agreed on – that is, that freedom of expression – saying what you think, within reason – is a necessary principle if people wish to talk to each other with a view to constructing a peaceful society together. Tolerating the absence of free speech displays a lack of appreciation of all others as independent-thinking, free beings. Not allowing individual persons to freely express themselves leads to their exclusion from the decision-making process.

- Thank you for your apology. You are probably right though in what you say – I would not go astray by displaying more backbone. Thinking all this through, I would like to summarise some facts as to where the absence of free expression would appear to lead. Jump in and interrupt anywhere you like....

Fact One is that my freedom of expression, and that of countless others, is curtailed by modern society. And Fact Two says that by not opposing this curtailment I am acquiescing to it. Fact Three says my woke culture obviously believes that some people should be heard over others or be freer than others to express themselves.

- And I can add the following to those facts. Fact Four is that in your woke cultural milieu, this exclusion is not random as it is only a certain type of person (that is, a victim of oppression) who is allowed freedom of expression. A further consequence is Fact Five – there must be a strong pull within your culture to behave as a victim, as one of the oppressed, as it is only victims who are permitted to express themselves freely. This seems to point to a further Fact Six – that there must be some elite persons or groups within society who decide on who the oppressed are.

- This leads necessarily to Fact Seven – among those valuable voices effectively excluded from speaking are those who may have genuine concern for the oppressed but who don't play the woke victimhood game, as well as those without any victim complex, and who bear their burdens in life bravely.

And, as I now see even more clearly, this leads to an un-pleasant Fact Eight: that this culture of exclusion of voices leaves us a long way removed from the democratic ideal. Only a certain few are heard, and very many voices, especially the communitarian types, are silenced.

– It certainly appears that way. I am glad you were able to analyse this for yourself – that is, losing freedom of expression ultimately leads to a loss of democracy.

I can show you a more direct logical route to that same conclusion, if you wish. Simply put, woke culture thinks that all institutions, viewed from the roots up, are systemically faulty and need to be radically overhauled. Democracy is one of those man-made institutions. Ergo, democracy needs a complete reworking.

At one level, change can be welcome: it can bring improvement. Returning to what the 1950s activist Peter Seeger said in *Turn-Turn-Turn:*

> To everything
>
> There is a season
>
> And a time to every purpose, under heaven.

We are in another season of change. It is fast-moving, and it may even be looked back on as being revolutionary. Change means that things can get better, but there is always the possibility that they will get worse. I would not like to see the result if our current change takes place in the absence of proper freedom of expression. Without such freedom there can never be genuine buy-in by those who are silenced – and thus excluded from participation in all decision-making.

When the winds of change blew in the 1960s, the western ship of freedom was deftly steered away from the rocks of communism under the flag of personal autonomy. Personal autonomy has led us into these new stormy waters, which are partially attributable to wokeness. The woke approach of setting societal groups against each other is exactly what one might expect from communism's little brother. If freedom of expression is restricted, along with other associated freedoms, I don't see anything to help steer us out of these dangerous waters.

Anyway, important as all this is, the possible demise of democracy is not exactly what I wanted to talk to you about.

- Hold on there now! You originally said there was no agenda, that we were simply having a conversation. Are you implying now that there is one, that there are things you wish to talk about? Are you feeling that having prised me open I am ready for the taking?

- Well, there was no agenda initially other than to talk about what we had agreed, which was to talk about talking.

But it was you who then steered us into deeper waters.

It was you who ascertained that it was your culture that sought to impose silence on you.

It was you who subsequently confirmed that your experience of our conversation has been positive – you 'were glad' we had it – it had affirmed for you that our talking together was a good thing.

It was you, on the way to that conclusion, who unearthed a deficiency in your culture: and it was you who explained how your culture does not appreciate free expression, and that this is undermining democracy.

Together we have agreed that free discussion cannot be allowed to become a disposable option for society – historically, it has been elevated as one of democracy's highest goods because it has proven its necessity.

Unearthing that final valuable insight through conversation alone should be enough to assure you that talking to each other is a necessary good. So why continue to build barriers? Why have no-go zones? Why not explore the full truth and reality of things?

- Truth? You mean truth versus falsehood, black versus white, good versus bad. If you don't mind me saying it – I am sure you do, but I am going to say it anyway – the use of that term sounds like you are being judgmental again.

But before this leads to another argument between us, and in the name of truth, I need to confess a further reason why I was reluctant to talk to you. My primary reason stemmed from a culturally generated anxiety that anything I said could be misunderstood, or be misconstrued, or could end up being quoted out of turn, resulting in some penalty, such as my being excluded or cancelled from mainstream discussion. The other reason – which maybe you won't like to hear – is that I know what you are going to say to me.

So, I would like you to be clear on this. I don't want to hear your negative judgements! I don't want you to be evaluating me! I don't want to hear of any agendas you might have for these exchanges of ours.

- 'You know what I am going to say to you?' Really? That makes you sound like a cultural snob, a know-it-all, someone whose mind is closed to alternative reasoning.

Or worse, perhaps it is woke-speak? Since I represent my class then I only can speak the narrative of that class, ergo, you know what I am going to say.

I don't know which is a worse fault!

I should warn you that you need to be wary of both those mentalities as either will make you an ideal victim for social media giants. Media platforms love snaring people who think they know it all or who have their own fixed views, as their algorithms can send such people down endless rabbit-holes occupied by like-minded others, ensuring their time-frittering commercial engagement with the platform. And the strange thing is, both people on the left and on the right of the political spectrum think that this only happens to the other side, whereas all are victims.

You need an open mind, not a closed one.

- You are so analytical! This is non-stop judgementalism now! You cannot really stop, can you?

- I can and I will. Conversations or dialogues like this one are an opportunity to clarify ideas. Once a discussion moves out of the shallows and beyond the banal and nonconsequential, it invariably moves into areas of judgement, of true and false, of right or wrong. At some stage you will have to acknowledge that judgements are worthwhile in that they are pointers in the direction of truth. As we said, there are times and seasons for everything. Now is one such time for you:

> A time to gain, a time to lose
>
> A time to rend, a time to sew
>
> A time for love, a time for hate...

Now is your time to gain and to win! I do apologise again, but you should have known I was bound to become judgemental once you accused me of negativity. But I will not analyse you any further.

Let's simply continue to talk about talking, as we were making good progress together on that front. We both agree about the significance of freedom of expression, so I would like us to explore that even further. I would like to tell you now why I think it is so important.

We have already concluded together that without it there can be no true consensus and thus democracy is substantially undermined. But is that fully true? Does society need to hear everyone's view in order to function? Can we not just use opinion polls and focus groups to find out what people think? Are any messages truly lost by restricting freedom of speech or expression? Is it really of such momentous value to allow people the freedom to sound off or is it purely a convenience that has worked well for our society?

- This is beginning to sound as if it is your turn to provide me with a monologue. I will settle for that. But please, avoid judging me!

TRYING TO REACH THE FUTURE THOUGH THE PAST

A monologue on a very modern detective story that, although there is continued uncertainty associated with the outcome, highlights the pre-eminence of truth. Freedom of expression sought to facilitate the search, allowing truth the opportunity to reveal itself.

Although I resort to generalities at times, I am most at home in dealing with firm facts, the specifics of things. I hope you therefore will allow me to work from the specific to the general in exploring this topic, that is, the necessity and power of free expression.

Origins of a virus

The Covid-19 pandemic provided the Western world with an enormous scare. For developing countries where the loss of life may have been comparatively greater, it became but another problem piled on top of existing ones. But for the West, Covid-19 undermined all its certainties – initially it even appeared that the virus might overwhelm all its highly-developed health services. It took a series of strategic lockdowns over long periods of time to restore calm to Western health systems.

Where did this virus come from? How can we ensure that such a pandemic does not happen again? For the general good of humanity, we need to know the answers to these questions. As scientists are good at their jobs, tracing the source of the virus should have been relatively easy. The very earliest indications were that it was a virus that had been enhanced in a laboratory and was released or had escaped. There are scientists who absolutely know the truth of this because of their involvement in work that may have led to the development of this virus. There are other scientists who know their virology well and can, with high degrees of certainty, trace its origins. (For example, the gene sequencing of the virus revealed the potentially suspicious presence of a previously patented gene sequence). Despite the existence of such possible scientific knowledge, over two years on, all indications would continue to appear to be inconclusive.

Uncovering truth

Much like the child who has thrown the stone that breaks a window, the embarrassing truth may need to be withheld from others. When the child protests – nobody threw any stones! – and CCTV says otherwise, the truth will out. Not so regarding this virus's origins, because the adults involved have powerful friends who can manage to neuter any CCTV equivalents. There are powerful international groups who have financed the laboratory work; there are vested interests in other laboratories who wish to continue to perform risk-laden, 'gain of function' experiments, there are major political interests and there is an embarrassment factor that might lead to trust in scientific research being undermined.

Thankfully however, we – in all our progressiveness – have ways to expose any such dishonesty, should it ever happen. We have scientific journals committed to the highest standards, we have our Western media that speak truth to power, and we have the greatest social communications networks the world has ever known, run by the top minds in the world.

Alas, one by one, these systems spectacularly failed us. Scientific journals have paymasters who assiduously seek to manage what is published – especially where there may be political implications – these initially only allowed articles that poured cold water on the hypothesis that the efficacy of the new virus was due to human intervention. We were assured, without any of the traditional proof that accompanied the exposure of origins of deadly past viruses, that the SARS-CoV-2 virus could not have come from a lab. Our Western news media abjectly failed to follow the trail of scientific breadcrumbs strewn before them by reputable independent commentators and scientists, presumably for a mixture of political and financial reasons. Social media moguls actively suppressed all those people who claimed valuable insights – this suppression incited by national security concerns or perhaps some other unspoken good – and created a climate whereby the 'lab-leak hypothesis' as it has come to be known, became fake news.

Martyrs for the cause

In the end, the persistence of scientific and journalistic martyrs paid off and a more truthful narrative is eventually emerging. We have the story now, we think. Reputable journals continue to use unscientific terms like 'fifty-fifty' to describe the probability of origin, alongside such ideas as there being a one in three-trillion chance that certain elements of the gene sequencing have arisen by natural evolution. Yet, even if we can attain a 99%-plus scientific certainty on the true story of virus origins, it still may never be within the interest of certain powers, be these political or scientific, to concede the complete truth to us. At least we know what we know: that is, the overwhelming scientific evidence continues to point to a still, publicly unacknowledged, and unproven lab-leak.

So what, you ask?

Well, by its continuous searching, our society displayed that it wanted to know the truth of things. There were some people who may have known the truth but worked hard to put a lid on it. Academics were silenced. Papers were not published. Social media platforms all took sides (or more correctly, the same side!). All the while, the generality of society showed

that it was dissatisfied hearing viewpoints. What it wanted was truth –
while others displayed a matching keenness that the same truth be hidden.

There are some who consider the world as comprising of themselves,
that is, the higher-ups or elites, and the little people. For the elites the
considerations and judgements of the latter never count. It is all because
the 'plain folk' are never smart enough to truly understand or appreciate
what is going on. The dripping sarcasm of Paul Brady's plaintive ballad *The
Island*, although addressing part of Ireland's painful recent past, captures
our present-day dilemma on being told that black is white, on not being
allowed to consider evidence to be what it is, even when it is as plain as
the nose on our face:

> Now I know us plain folks don't see all the story.
>
> And I know this peace and love's just copping out.
>
> And I guess these young boys dying in the ditches.
>
> Is just what being free is all about.
>
> And how this twisted wreckage down on main street.
>
> Will bring us all together in the end.
>
> And we'll go marching down the road to freedom....

In short, all sides know that there is a truth, and everyone has either a
positive or negative disposition towards it. Most plain folk want to know
what happened and how it happened, aware that true knowledge could
provide a solid foundation in looking to future actions or decisions that
might be taken. Scientific elites have other agendas and so must carefully
manage our access to the truth, lest it upend important plans.

Truth helps

Is it important that we know? Yes, humanity is on the move, straining forward, like an explorer entering the unknown, always looking to the future, and watching out for false signals that may lead it astray. With each step humanity takes, it wants to place its feet on firm ground. It is truth that sustains it and allows it to move forward. Without truth humanity may still coalesce around some narrative – the urge to unify pushing humankind on, but then perhaps society builds on the shaky platform of a lie and will pay a later price for this.

By knowing the truth, we get to establish who was telling lies and covering up the truth – providing a better understanding of who can and cannot be trusted in the future, as well as highlighting the grounds on which such judgements can be made. Is that also important? Absolutely. Ultimately, all that we know we know through others. The last thing we need are lies, like excess mica in concrete, undermining the structure we build for ourselves.

What do we mean by truth in this case? Well, it is what has happened. Truth is when the narrative or story that is told conforms with the reality of things. We need to know the reality before we venture out. If our college is closed today, then we won't go there expecting it to be open. We will bring an umbrella if we are told that heavy rain is reasonably expected – otherwise we will leave it at home. We will instal useful safety measures if we are warned of a genuine hazard.

Truth is a vital ingredient in helping us make decisions and we need to be able to access it. The eminent 19th-century philosopher, John Stuart Mill, believed that enlightened judgment in society was possible only if one considered all facts and ideas, and tested one's own conclusions against opposing views, He believed that all ideas should be represented in society's 'marketplace of ideas.' Other democrats would argue that systems of self-government require that everyone is able to contribute, thus providing a proper checking function on any government excess. These arguments point to freedom of expression as being the climate in which truth can emerge.

Yet freedom of expression is not reducible to a statement of principle that all voices be heard, so that 'real' democracy happens. It is much more. It is the way that thoughts and beliefs get a public airing and tested for their validity. Its existence guarantees that potentially important ideas and voices are not silenced. It allows us the possibility of knowing if, and when, we are right, or wrong. It permits truth to exercise the prestige that it holds, and to freely circulate and win allegiance. It is an acknowl-edgment that truth is vitally important to us, that it is possible for us, in listening to others and in exchanging views, to ascertain the truth of things; that it is possible to present the truth, or to share it, with each oth-er; that truth has its own lustre; that when truth is recognised, it gives us confidence to take our next step. For the future is never predictable and the next step is always dependent on high quality information as to what lies ahead. All freedoms are accompanied by risks, for such is the human condition, yet the rewards are so much greater. Freedom of expression is a valuable tool that allows truth to reveal itself, permitting it to continue to sustain us on our journey.

LIVE MY LIFE AS IT'S MEANT TO BE

On how self-censorship is not a victimless act and why speaking out can be a necessity; why lies will persist if people do not stand up for truth and why not all people who tell lies are liars; why truth sides with reality and why science requires the oxygen of truth. Placing appropriate restrictions on social media platforms presupposes freedom of expression in negotiating the rules.

- Thanks for providing those cogent ideas on the impor-tance of accessing truth. I get great satisfaction in watching mystery thrillers and being able to work out 'who done it' using the clues presented. Even with such inconsequen-tial stories there comes a sense of freedom and satisfaction from knowing the full truth of things.

- I hope you appreciate that I avoided raising issues of right or wrong, and I did not seek to blame anyone as such. I presented the facts of the matter – I stated, for example, that the media did not follow the breadcrumbs, including the clues left by scientists in their email exchanges, allowing for the possibility that they may have had good reasons for their actions.

Aside from the facts of the matter, one might wish to consider the morality of what happened. That is to look at reality on another plane. It is a way of evaluating how freedom was exercised as events evolved. Why was one decision taken and not another? Why have we still not heard the full story? Should the media not have followed up on the clues better? Why did they not do so? Was any damage done as a result? These are all moral questions. I avoided making such judgements and sought to outline the facts, the reality as we know it.

First you have reality – things are – for example, the virus exists. Then you have truth – the accurate recognition of that reality, which is different than falsehood – such as for example: you are only imagining it, there is no virus. In the light of truth we can then examine how freedom was exercised, for example, the rights and wrongs of any human actions that may have been involved in introducing the virus to the world – this is what morality is concerned with.

Without a proper recognition of reality, without truth, one cannot safely take one's next step in the world. Each person needs to know whether there is a deep chasm or solid ground in front of them before they take their next step. They need to know if they are exercising their freedom wisely. In the case of the Covid virus, a timely truth was of enormous significance – justifying the application of moral brakes to certain scientific research, or alternatively, if a fully natural virus, then galvanising further research so that we are better equipped when the next deadly virus comes along. Without truth, it having found itself replaced by an excess of clever words, we march forward with deep uncertainty.

- You used a word that made me flinch. It is one that I understand in a religious context but seldom hear it used in a secular one – that is, you spoke of martyrs. By it I presume that you mean people who stand by what they know to true despite all the obstacles. Jordan Peterson promotes this idea that there is nothing more adventurous than telling the truth! And most people will agree that there is no more noble witness than someone who stands by his professional learning to defend truths that emerge, especially in the face of commercial or political opposition which often can be arrayed in professional robes.

This got me to thinking about my own self-censorship. As I confessed earlier, I don't always stand by what I think, even though I often am convinced of its truth. There are many of my peers who, in the name of seeking justice for others, or in seeking to ensure others would not be offended or would not feel judged, tell me to keep my ideas to myself. Certainly, many viewpoints I have will be upsetting to someone, somewhere. Several peers will even go as far as to say that my opinions, the words I express, are hurtful – claiming that some words are violence! In response to this or even in anticipation of it, I censor myself.

While I leave myself open to the claim of overdramatising,

I feel I live a life akin to the family in the horror movie *A Quiet Place*. This film is about a repressive silence forced on a family seeking to escape terrifying aliens. The aliens sense their prey by the sounds they make. Speaking one's mind or expressing politically unacceptable truths making one prey to long-term or short-term public humiliation at the hands of those who may intensely dislike hearing what has been said. Silence is often the safer option.

It's not only me that suppresses truth in this way. The tech giants also censor people's accounts in the name of not offending others, even though what is being said may be patently true. They are often selective in whose viewpoints they suppress, as if the social media platforms have established that certain groups or viewpoints must be protected.

According to you, if one does not stand by truth, it never gets properly recognised in society and so society can go astray. If I understand you correctly you are saying that if the truth hurts, then so what, but that it should not be suppressed.

- Yes. If the truth hurts that is unfortunate, but a greater misfortune can result if it is not heard. If society is not using truth as its beacon, then it will end up being led by falsehood, with whatever consequences that entails. Such lies were at the heart of the countless millions of lives lost to 20th century ideologies. Aleksandr Solzhenitsyn in his writings speaks strongly of how those under communist rule were constantly forced to live out a lie. In Russia, under communism, the penalty for speaking the truth was, at a minimum, social or political ostracisation, but more likely it led, as in Solzhenitsyn's case, to a hard-labour sentence in a work camp, or to a death sentence.

There are times when some form of self-censorship may be required, as one does not always have to express a view. Basic decency requires that we do not set out to offend people, even if we think their newly acquired tattoo or hairstyle is stupid. We must have some rules for social engagement.

At the same time, truth must be upheld, otherwise it disappears, and we no longer have the required compass to help us avoid sinking in a swamp of lies and deceit. Self-censorship is not a victimless act.

There probably was a time in the past when one could speak in generalities about a social problem without being accused of denigrating a group or class of people. That is not so nowadays. For example, there are many potential solutions to problems of poverty, mental health, race, migration or gender issues that cannot be spoken about without been deemed racist, colonialist, homophobic, genderphobic, misogynist or whatever. People, especially educators, in colleges, schools, workplaces and on social media can feel as if they are threading on eggshells. One incorrect step, one misspoken word and their reputation or livelihood can be endangered. If they are perceived as influencers, they may find themselves banished to the darkness, with no trial or judge or jury, due to the baying of woke elites within society.

The official responses to Covid, as contrasted with the suppressed viewpoints, captures completely the point I wish to make. There was one primary Covid narrative allowed – that it was a highly dangerous virus, and that vaccines were the only solution. No matter how prestigious their credentials were, anyone who suggested that lockdowns were an overreaction, that the Covid death numbers were exaggerated and needed to be stratified according to age, that there were worthwhile treatments which were being ignored, and that the dangers of vaccines were not properly acknowledged, was dispatched to the darkness of professional anonymity.

Unfortunately, then, the luxury of saying things as they really are – that is, of speaking the truth – is not as available to us as we might wish. I suppose then your use of the word 'martyr', as one who is ready to take the risk for the good of all, is an appropriate one.

- True, but by using the term martyr I don't want you to think that I am suggesting that such actions should be uncommon – as true martyrs often are as rare as hens' teeth! You tell me that you don't have the luxury of saying things as they really are. I say to you that your society cannot afford the luxury of you not doing so.

You would do well to read why Winston Marshall, a member of that immensely popular band, Mumford and Son, left the band at the height of his career. He loved what he was doing, producing songs with messages of hope and love, and he enjoyed what he saw as an exhilarating career. He had tweeted support for someone whom he regarded as a brave author for recently producing a book on left-wing violence. From then on, a Twitter censor mob came after Marshall. Rather than inflict misery on his band colleagues by standing his professional ground, thus dragging them into his fight for truth, he retired from a career he loved.

His reason – he saw that by not continuing to support a brave journalist who was promulgating the truth about extremism would be to participate in the lie that such extremism did not exist, or worse, that it was a force for good. As Marshall said himself, 'I could remain (with the band) and continue to self-censor, but it will erode my sense of integrity. Gnaw my conscience. I've already felt that beginning.'

More people like Winston Marshall are needed to stand up for truth, people who will not acquiesce to the lie. Returning again to Aleksandr Solzhenitsyn who encourages such actions: 'You can resolve to live your life with integrity. Let your credo be this: Let the lie come into the world, let it even triumph. But not through me.'

- I am concerned that as we speak, we seem to be aligning truth with one side (can I say 'our' side?) and attributing lies to the other side. I know that when I tell a lie I feel a sense of shame. Surely others sense that also, and if so, how can someone persist in lying?

And are we really saying that committed woke people are persistent liars? I don't buy that, as many are genuine people with real concerns. Perhaps they can be over the top in expressing their apprehensions, but I don't think they are liars. I have green friends who are so concerned about the planet that they are fearful of bringing children into the world, and others who believe that to be childless is a sacrifice they must make for the planet. Having been told that the single most effective action anyone can take to help reduce CO2 emissions is to have one fewer child, some people are responding by making such personal sacrifices. There is even a small measurable climate vasectomy effect in advanced countries! You cannot dismiss as liars those people who are ready to make such sacrifices, who put their money where their mouth is.

- That's a very good point. I accept that there are real people with real concerns who have adopted a woke culture. Society needs people to be concerned to make society better. But if improvement is to come about, their analyses and diagnoses of the problems must be right. Mumford and Son have a song *The Cave* that sheds light on that dilemma. The song is based on an allegory of the ancient Greek philosopher, Plato. Plato's Cave tells of prisoners who from childbirth are shackled deep within a cave, unable to move their heads and forced to look only at the wall directly in front of them. Behind them there is a platform, and behind that, a fire. Figures – prison guards – walk and interact with objects on the platform, and the light from the fire projects their shadows onto the wall. For the prisoners, the shadows they see on the wall are reality, these being the only things they have ever witnessed. One prisoner, on breaking free, sees the workings of the fire behind him and then realises his idea of reality was a mere illusion. Despite his fear he continues exploring and eventually emerges into the sunlight outside of the cave, where all truth is revealed to him. He then returns to inform all his fellow prisoners as to what is outside in the real world.

Truth is the measure of an underlying reality. The reality in this story is outside the cave, although those within the cave are deceived into thinking otherwise. There are some in our world from whom the truth has been hidden – as they have never been allowed to explore beyond the cave wall. And there are others who will continue to insist that the narrative within the cave is true because they don't really accept the idea of objective reality and insist that all reality is created by the individual.

Just saying that something is so does not make it true; it must be linked to reality. When you say – for example, 'I love you' – it is not just your expression of the words that brings this love about, there needs to be an existing underlying inner reality to the words that makes them true. Thus, if you have shown your love in various actions before making the declaration, then it is these realities that imbue the spoken words with meaning and testify to the truthfulness of your expression.

Many people today have lost that anchor with what is real. They believe that it is language itself that creates the reality, much in the same way as Plato's cave dwellers believe that the shadows are what is real. They think that by making the 'I love you' statement that they are making the reality happen. If you were to say to such people that a man cannot become a woman, they will argue that it is you who is denying a man his freedom to become a woman. They believe the power lies in the language and not in the underlying reality. For them, language is the means to create change.

That is a dangerous trap and one that is much easier for secularists to fall into than for Christians. Humans explain things to each other by stories. Some stories are true, that is, those which have an underlying reality to them. Others are false because these don't relate to reality. People need to be able to distinguish what is real from what is a fictitious statement. True and false are grounded in our reason and in our human nature. Secularists don't have these anchors for true and false, nor for right and wrong – as the scope of their reason is truncated, and for them human nature is a mere creation of the minds of human beings. When everything is a social construct, then almost anything can become a true statement simply by people asserting it to be the case.

In this prevailing climate it would be wrong then to claim that all people who tell lies – who state things to be true that are not – are liars. They may think by asserting something to be true that it becomes true, so they are not setting out to deceive but to create. It is that they live in a make-believe world in which what they assert to be true magically becomes true. Their claims may be lies, but they don't see that and consequently they don't experience the same sense of guilt about it. What you need to do is to educate them into the reality of things, to move them beyond make-believe, to seek to ground them in the reality of human nature and reason. Mumford and Son make such a plea on behalf of the cave dweller:

Now let me at the truth

Which will refresh my broken mind...

'Cause I need freedom now

And I need to know how

To live my life as it's meant to be.

In this way, the truth, they imply, will begin to set him free:

And I'll find strength in pain

And I will change my ways

I'll know my name as it's called again.

- I would like to return to the censorship question. What about that censorship that is conducted by the all-knowing tech-giants? Is that ever acceptable?

- It may be helpful to look again at the example of the search for the source for the Covid virus – was it or was it not a lab-enhanced virus? At the heart of this matter there is a black and white issue that cannot be obfuscated. The tech giants – for no transparent reason – chose, from early on, to actively suppress those people who were advancing the 'lab-leak' hypothesis. In retrospect, this was a very dangerous act – it denied society access to vital information that might have been helpful in reducing the virus's evolutionary spread, as well as access to knowledge on how best to combat future virus-driven pandemics.

The establishment of social media platforms has allowed us to communicate very efficiently with each other. To a large degree these have displaced the means of communication we might otherwise have used. For example, the rise of WhatsApp groups has displaced most text messaging. People have become dependent on these new methods of communication. The platforms were initially understood to be neutral spaces, like public noticeboards, operating within normal legal constraints. Yet they don't operate as neutral spaces and have shown themselves to be prone to high degrees of politicisation. There are widespread reports that their algorithms have denied space for truth-telling, sometimes with ruthless efficiency. Certain 'chosen' persons have acquired greater speaking rights than others, whereas certain other views are not allowed the oxygen of publicity. Too often, under the name of disinformation, many truth-telling viewpoints are suppressed. The monopoly-like power that these platforms have acquired has enhanced the impact of the very public judgments they make on who is, or who is not, to be trusted. By their suppressive wisdom they suggest that some truth tellers are charlatans. They even would appear to have the power to determine who should or should not rule in any country. They can suppress true news items for months on end that can impact on elections, as the New York Post found out with its famous laptop story in October 2020. This was suppressed by Twitter and Facebook and thus ignored by other outlets, and subsequently many months later (when the truth may have mattered less) was validated as true. Social media giants can suppress national presidents for expressing unwelcome political views. They can adjust their rules in an ad hoc manner to affect international hostilities. They can even suppress negative views about their own social media platforms that might otherwise undermine their perceived value to society. What could be more corrosive of truth and freedom?

Science has become one of their many victims. The world is sold on the great value of science. As podcaster and biologist, Bret Weinstein, insists, science advances by first proposing a hypothesis, then testing it, then the possible confirmation or refinement of the hypothesis leading it to become a theory. Big tech interferes with scientific advancement by politically choosing to advance or promote one narrative over another, which is a potential means of subverting truth, with damaging consequences. In inappropriately taking sides, big tech subverts the natural order of scientific progress. By becoming involved in a partisan manner, the side it takes will silence or swamp the opposing voice. With such management of social media platforms, big tech actively involves itself in the destruction of dissent and seeks to create a manufactured consent. That big tech should silence a world-renowned 180-year-old scientific journal *(The BMJ)* for an article questioning the clinical Covid-vaccine trials conducted by Pfizer, without giving adequate grounds for doing so, is a clear case of an abuse of power.

Big tech also behaves in a similar manner with other branches of human industry, including politics, where ideas need to be properly challenged and tested. When, in modern-day Canada, fundraising platforms try to sequester donations because they don't like the views of a political movement, or banks deselect their customers due to political pressures, this is a far cry from democratic ideals. Big-tech and social media platforms urgently need some rules of engagement, ones that do not allow them to be so dismissive of truth, nor of the freedom of others to search for it.

In a reference to George Orwell's famous futuristic novel *1984*, where a state ministry was tasked with providing propaganda and rewriting history, billionaire investor Peter Thiel, a then director of Meta, claimed that he personally would take 'QAnon and Pizza-gate conspiracy theories any day over a Ministry of Truth.'

-   I take your message, loud and clear. In selecting what news it tells you, big tech is really messing with your mind. Maybe Meta's most honest move in recent times has been to re-brand its 'News Feed' simply as 'Feed'! Through exercising its capacity to suppress valid news stories and viewpoints, big tech is creating enormous unsolvable problems for society. While social media's unwelcome psychological influence on young teenagers is often acknowledged, we have yet to fully appreciate the degree to which it is shaping minds throughout the whole of society. Crowd psychologists are not agreed on whether mass formation psychosis exists, or whether social media could have that impact, but the vigour associated with Covid control measures, and their ease of implementation, raises legitimate questions as to whether big tech can hasten the advent of totalitarianism. Simply put, big tech has the tools at hand to create any outcome it wishes in our modern democratic society. If I really support freedom of expression, then I should neither condone the censorship currently happening across social media nor should I self-censor.

But, apart from seeking controls on big tech's suppressive tendencies, should each social media platform not be allowed to have rules for their own users? These are private businesses, with their own ethos. Can platforms really be expected to become a free-for-all? Surely there needs to be rules of engagement as each platform sees fit.

- Great damage co-exists alongside the great good provided by social media. For example, anxiety disorders, such as anorexia (a fear of gaining weight) at one end of a scale and bigorexia (obsessing about being inadequately muscular) at the other end, are fuelled by social media engagement. Gaming addictions and gambling addictions are similarly destructively enhanced by social media use. So, rules of engagement must be hammered out for social media platforms in a whole range of areas, and not solely with regard to the exercise of free speech. And rules should apply equally to all – during the Russian invasion of Ukraine some social media companies seemed to think it was ok to tolerate hatred from one side but not from the other. However, the productive implementation of such rules can only be attained where there is true freedom of expression in the very process of forming them.

In Ireland, a 2022 review of abortion legislation began with meetings with chosen stakeholders, all of whom were pro-abortion voices – such a clear exclusion of widely-held alternative viewpoints undermines the very notion of a democratic society. There will be different viewpoints, and these must get a fair hearing. A similar political polarisation exists on issues around free speech on social media platforms – on one side there is the cancel culture, and on the other, there is a libertarian overemphasis on the individual – and this division can thwart any discussion around regulation. But for social media regulation to be effective, freedom of expression for all must inform all parts of the process. Additionally, this freedom must be appreciated as a principle undergirding any regulations that may be adopted.

I am not claiming, as some may do, that freedom on social media platforms should be unlimited – the platforms themselves will argue that your right to free speech cannot be interpreted as a right to broadcast your views on their platforms. Most non-partisan people will agree that Russian disinformation efforts that have been used as a tool of war in Syria and also in the Ukraine cannot be allowed to hide under a free-speech mantle. The use of deep-fake tactics, as for example during wartime, should not be tolerated by media platforms. Yet, on the other hand, the big tech silencing of all social media voices that questioned the EU-NATO war narrative on Ukraine created a deeply unhelpful censorious attitude that only assisted the arms industry. People are entitled to access informed views beyond any tailored official narrative. Since free expression is such a fundamental freedom linked to our nature as social beings, then any restriction on it must be fully justifiable. We have the freedom because we have the duty to live in peace and harmony with each other.

Gossip is an unfortunate side effect of free speech, as is lying, yet we tolerate these, within certain limits, in the name of the greater good. The amplification of gossip, and lies, may be the price that must be paid is we are to avoid the partisan restriction of views.

Happily, there are still some actions that practically everyone in society agrees are wrong and that should not be given any oxygen. Controls are needed where there is significant evidence of damage done in society by specific groups. That seems obvious with child pornography or indeed with pornography more generally. Also, controls are required on gambling apps that use sophisticated psychological techniques to capture those with a potential gambling addiction. Or indeed we must avoid the Pandora's box that will be opened should gaming companies share personal data with gambling companies. There are also many issues on how social media apps can psychologically manipulate young minds for economic gain. Yet, as time goes by, societal consensus on most moral issues seems to be disappearing, at least at the level of political decision makers.

Despite numerous opportunities to limit the widely acknowledged, damaging effects of extreme pornography, policy makers never respond. In many ways, political elites appear more trapped by a prevailing culture than are ordinary citizens. The Russian invasion of Ukraine was regarded by ordinary European citizens as a brazen affront to all values, but it took some days for European leaders to fully come around to that viewpoint and then they only very gradually imposed serious sanctions on Russia.

In a democratic society, the rules that are adopted need to result from a consensual approach and not be the product of some influential elites who have the power to swing the majority to their side. And I say consensual since democracy should not be reduced to the majority suppressing the views of the minority. If the social media companies were smaller (or if they had not been allowed to grow to the degree that they occupy a dominant market share) or if there was true ideological competition between them, then it might make sense for them to continue to make their own rules. But given the dominance nowadays of a small number of players in this global communications space, and the monopolistic powers they hold, I do not think that they, as private businesses, can hide away from public scrutiny or regulation – we have gone a long way beyond that point now.

- You seem to be suggesting then that it would be better for national governments to make the rules of engagement for platforms?

-   Yes, just as these make libel and defamation laws. The proposed new EU Digital Services Act appears to be a worthwhile response, although it raises the alarming spectre of 'disinformation' being used to suppress free speech or the term 'hate' being deliberately and inappropriately applied. That thirty- five civil liberties groups across Europe have come together to oppose an EU proposal to oblige all platforms to scan all private digital correspondence (dubbed 'chat control') shows that there are strong controlling authoritarian tendencies at play at EU Commission level. The Digital Services legislation itself promises tough consequences for platforms and websites that host banned content such as hate speech, disinformation or child sexual abuse images. The stated objective is to make what is illegal offline to be illegal online, but it may yet extend to material deemed as 'legal but harmful' much like the British Online Safety Bill, which is making its way through the Westminster Parliament. Notwithstanding this Bill's merits, by giving specific powers to politicians over freedom of speech, and by using broad definitions as to what constitutes hate, it has the capacity to create a chill factor on free expression. Whither the future of comedy halls and satire? The latest half-baked US response was the establishment of a Disinformation Governance Board, dubbed by sceptics as the 'Ministry of Truth', as it was established immediately after Elon Musk made a takeover offer for Twitter. This political move, allied with the Department of Homeland Security deeming malinformation as terrorism, has libertarians and conservatives alike concerned about the capacity of inappropriate censorship of legitimate anti-government views.

Political opposition succeeded in 'pausing' the establishment of the Board, having convinced the general public for now that disinformation lies in the eyes of the beholder. Having elements of the security state, specialists in disinformation, controlling social media discourse sounds Orwellian because it is.

Not all censorship is inherently negative. Sweden has recently set up a new agency, dubbed by some as a 'Ministry of Truth'. The Swedish Psychological Defense Agency aims to combat election disinformation and undue election influence. Its website states that 'we defend our open and democratic society and free opinions by identifying, analysing and responding to inappropriate influences and other misleading information directed at Sweden or Swedish interests.' The agency will 'offer support to agencies, municipalities, regions, companies and organisations and contribute to strengthening resilience within our population.' Undoubtedly, a country may need to protect itself against foreign influence in its elections via social media, but there a tightrope to be walked on the issue of censorship and in ensuring that such agencies are not used to suppress uncomfortable internal political viewpoints. Controls can be agreed consensually but then there is a genuine political need for controls on the controllers!

When billionaire Elon Musk purchased Twitter, he highlighted how platforms could respect freedom, while operating within the law. Musk expressed the importance of social media platforms being inclusive arenas for free speech. For him, people should have both the reality and perception that they can speak freely within the bounds of the law. He proposed that Twitter's algorithm be open sourced and that any action taken against tweets be thoroughly explained to the public to avoid behind-the-scenes manipulation on the platform by the company. "My strong intuitive sense is that having a public platform that is maximally trusted and broadly inclusive is extremely important to the future of civilization," Musk said.

- I note we are back speaking about controls and rules again, but we have yet to establish ground rules for our very own conversation. I accept that until now I have only expressed reluctance. Perhaps I am ready to accept some sort of agenda, if you wish to propose one?

- Well, you yourself have established the most basic ground rule – that we need to learn to trust each other. By agreeing to have this dialogue you expressed your trust in me, and, naturally, I also trust you. You yourself even said that the way to get through to woke warriors was by seeking to establish mutual trust.

What exactly does trust mean? It is to build truth in a relationship, and for it to be seen as such by both. We know that in our exchanges there may be some uncomfortable moments, but we are both in agreement that we won't lie to each other.

Truth is not something that can be taken for granted. Some people can get angry about it and try to evade it because it makes them uncomfortable – truth can be a very demanding master!

- I don't think you should be surprised to encounter anger in exchanges, as you have seen with me. People who are confused can get upset and angry. For example, my generation are confused about truth. We talk about 'my' truth, what is true for me, and not of truth as something that is out there, independent of how we might feel about it. We think we all have our different versions of truth – what is true for one need not be true for another. When someone then comes along and talks of something being *really* true that can cause others to be angry in that they see their truth being challenged.

- You raise a good point that I overlooked. When I talk about truth I mean an objective reality, something that is outside and beyond the person, something outside the cave, something that the person can grasp. Many in your generation speak as if truth was subject to their way of looking at the world. On the other hand, sometimes a claim to know objective truth is viewed as bigotry by others, as it may directly challenge their version of truth. No wonder they get angry! I think we need to take another breather in this dialogue to allow me to embark on a monologue as to where truth fits into the lives of human beings.

- That would be very helpful. It is funny how very few people today are ready to address these deeper questions of life. Whereas young people of my generation have a sense of being someone, and a strong sense of self, they hold on to it in a self-reflective, narcissistic way. They have a poor idea of who or what that self is about, or one's inter-relationship with others. School Wellbeing programmes promote self-centredness. In advocating self-improvement there is an emphasis on how others might view the person themselves rather than promoting an interest in others as 'other'. A well-known joke accurately reflects this: 'Enough about my narcissistic talking about myself. Now, you tell me what you think of me?' These programmes seldom delve into who or what it means to be human or seek to understand human persons in all their beauty and ugliness. In pre-medieval times people were wrongly taught that our planet Earth was the centre of the universe, whereas nowadays we are wrongly taught that it is we, the individual person, that is at the centre! We have made so little progress, it would seem.

I know this is a wider question, but maybe you need to answer it first for me – who or what are human beings? If I had a better grasp of that perhaps then I might see where truth fits in?

- You are right. Mumford and Son agree that it is important to know who you are, and not live life in the cave:

> So come out of your cave walking on your hands
>
> And see the world hanging upside down
>
> You can understand dependence
>
> When you know the maker's hand.

My monologue will seek to enlighten you.

ARE WE HUMAN OR ARE WE DANCER?

A monologue contrasting the cold secular logic which presents to us the self-made person – the dancer – with the Christian worldview of a creature freely seeking to understand one's objective evolutionary greatness – the human.

What a piece of work is a man!

How noble in reason, how infinite in faculty!

In form and moving how express and admirable!

In action how like an angel, in apprehension how like a god!

The beauty of the world. The paragon of animals.

And yet, to me, what is this quintessence of dust?

Thus flows Shakespeare's attempt to fathom the complexity of man. Layer upon layer of evolutionary complexity has somehow brought about the rational creatures that humans are today. But who or what are human beings? How do they function? What is their purpose? What is human life all about? These are what one might call foundational questions.

Meaning and purpose

Viktor Frankl's personal experience of Nazi death camps confirmed con-
clusively for him that the people who survived the incredible hardship
of the extermination camps were those who had meaning and purpose
in their lives – that meaning often being expressed in love for a significant other, for example, a spouse or another family member. Modern-day
public intellectuals like Jordan Petersen agree that young people seek
meaning in their lives, and it is this that propels them forward.

Given the importance of foundational questions, it would seem reasonable that our public culture would continually concern itself with these,
as answers empower people. Unfortunately, despite the best efforts of
people like Peterson, most questioning as to meaning and purpose is off
the agenda of Western culture. Even our philosophers today get bogged
down in reductive thinking and the semantics of language and feel unable
to ask fundamental questions as to the meaning and purpose of man. To
explain this negligence, I need to revisit in more detail some aspects of
the worldviews you mentioned earlier.

The impact of secularism

Since the foundation of the modern democratic state, secularism has
gradually sought to push Christianity to the side-lines within the culture.
Over the past few generations, the logic of secularism has taken a firm
hold in society causing society to avoid what it sees as 'unanswerable'
fundamental questions and thus leading to the resulting confusions of
the present day.

Meaning and purpose are at the heart of a religious outlook. As you are
aware, the Christian worldview proposes that human beings are a special

creation of God, that humankind has fallen in some way (original sin) and that God sent his Son to redeem us, so that on death we can join him again, for eternity. God's human creatures are made of matter and spirit, are all loved by God, and all have an eternal destiny. That destiny is best pursued by loving God and loving one's fellow humans. While Christianity has more to add to these details, this basic understanding of human purpose also finds strong echoes in other religions. Early pre-Christian Greek philosophers such as Aristotle and Plato had no doubt that the universe owed its existence to a creator, God.

Secularism sees things differently. For it, God is either irrelevant or he does not exist. For years, in the day-to-day functioning of society this secularist approach made little practical impact on people's lives as many societal structures were infused with the Christian worldview. Now, after many generations, with this Christian understanding for the most part expunged, the secular understanding has taken a strong hold, and its logic prevails.

Secularism, in holding that there is no God, sees no purpose and meaning for humankind beyond the individual person themselves. Humans are random cosmic dust particles that have developed and evolved into what they are today. Reality is what they create for themselves. They obviously have sense appetites and reason, so these can be used to help answer life's questions. Each person has a sense, an impulse to freedom, which should be maximised as best one can, and therein one will find happiness and fulfilment.

For secularism the only truths, that is, things one can be sure of as real, are those that can be measured by empirical science – that is, by using logic and one's senses, one can come to know things. Nothing beyond that is knowable. Knowability, the truth of things, is thus confined to that which can be empirically or scientifically measured. There is no point in asking any big questions on the why of life, because there is no way of answering these!

Despite an inherent foundational flaw in this secular way of thinking – its fundamental principle as to what can be known cannot be proven to be true – this principle nonetheless dominates secularism's understanding of the world. In the secular worldview, there are no objective truths on which everyone must agree – everything (other than proven scientific facts) is subjective. For secularism there is nothing essential about the society humankind has put together – it could have come together in another way with different principles. Despite these weaknesses, secularism thrives, partly as its prestige is enormously boosted by the concurrent successes of science and of the free market in generating unforeseen wealth.

Secularism is an offshoot of Christianity, which also takes pride in a humanity's rational capacities. But secularism truncates reason to embrace empirical scientific reason only, effectively ignoring other ways of knowing, and in so doing destroys much of a person's self-understanding, denying one the capacity to know who he or she is. The full fruits of this narrow vision are being experienced today. One cannot escape considering the secular human person being like The Killers 'dancer', following a fixed cosmic dance routine written aeons ago or recently put together by talented choreographers who expect everyone to follow the set piece.

The secular worldview sees purpose as being made or invented by humanity itself. The person then uses reason to maximise his or her freedom and enjoyment. Thus, the secularist focus is on the autonomous individual seeking personal happiness, and only on others insofar as their freedom enhances that of the particular individual.

How Christianity views the world

This contrasts dramatically with the Christian worldview that emphasises that humans are created as free, interdependent beings who have a purpose; they are made to love and for love – and this reality should dominate all societal interactions. Thus, on the secular side we have free (or perhaps completely cosmically determined) individuals focused on what is best for them individually in the here and now, whereas on the Christian side we have interdependent persons, all with meaning and purpose, equal in the eyes of God, carving out a future that they can all help shape together.

Unfortunately, you will come across people, including in Ireland, whose minds are closed to any discussion influenced by Christian thought, severely limiting rational discussion of the type we are having now. Without arguing the genuine rights and wrongs of history, it is worthwhile pointing out that the grounds on which people often selectively condemn Ireland's Christian past – and use it as an excuse for closed minds – are because it has not been Christian enough, that Christians reneged on their Christian and human responsibilities. It is not usually the Christian message itself that is the obstacle to discussion, but rather the way it has been seen to have been lived out.

The impact on truth

Two different understandings of truth arise from these contrasting worldviews. For the secularist, there is no objective truth in this cosmic jungle, apart from that arising from scientific certainty. All other truth is supplied by humanity, it is subjective, and is worked out as we go along. For the Christian this is an intelligible world, which was created in a certain way and has truth as its lode star. For the Christian then, there is truth, for the secularist there is, predominantly, 'my' truth.

The secular worldview has now been pressed to its limit by post-modern ideas. With no God there is no objective truth, and everything is subjective, including one's personal identity. Any illusions or delusions a person may have about their identity must be recognised and accepted by others, otherwise they are implicitly denying that individual's identity and impinging on personal freedoms. The limitations on identity are no longer set by rationality and are ultimately determined by how much non-sense humanity is willing to tolerate at any given period. With reason deposed, it is the will which rules the roost. Recently, a Welsh university was ridiculed for encouraging staff to use a gender pronoun guide that included 'catgender' for people who identify as cats – in that particular establishment the guide subsequently underwent minor adaptation to make it more tolerable. There was no apology – the university likely adjudged itself as going a step too far, too soon.

With no God and no objective truth, language too loses its objectivity, and it is reduced to comprising of words with meanings that reflect the power plays taking place in society. The resulting lack of clarity in the use of language undermines proper communication – there can only be confusion. Nowadays, arguments made proposing the objectivity of language are seen in some secular circles as acts of bigotry.

With no God, there is no proper way to understand how the spiritual and physical person are interlinked. The human body, as some in the present secular culture maintain, is the enemy – one's biology may be telling lies.

This lack of understanding of the unity of body and spirit now rests at the root of current widespread 'gender equals sex' debate.

On the other hand, having God there makes everything so much clearer. There is an objective reality that can be described using objective language. There is a purposeful biological human nature with instructions for use. The human person has objective truth to guide him or her, and has rationality, senses, emotions, and history all helping in understanding who one is. Humans have freedoms that are fully tempered by consideration of the freedom of others. These freedoms are linked to their created reality as equal, free, and rational beings. Persons serve themselves and others best when they use these freedoms to seek and pursue the good that is written into their being. Happiness is to be found in interdependence and service, and not in self-isolation.

I hope you can see from this that the Christian worldview presents a complete vision of what it means to be human. Secularism, in side-lining Christianity, has obscured that vision for many in society (and has also shelved all visions of humankind's eternal destiny), ultimately removing humankind's sense of usefulness in the world, contributing to the anxiety and conflict we see today.

Are we happy with how the new secularism is now shaping us? Do we want to rediscover the freedom given to the flesh-and-blood, God-directed human being or are we happy moving in time with everyone else in the pre-determined chorus line, be it man-made or the fruit of cosmic determinism? Are we human or are we dancer?

Secularism, having lived on the emotionless logic of reason, is dying in its cold hands. The danger is that secularism may pull Western democracy down along with it unless society is revitalised with religious thought:

Are we human or are we dancer?

My sign is vital, my hands are cold

And I'm on my knees looking for the answer

Are we human or are we dancer?

IF I DIDN'T HAVE YOUR LOVE

It is God, as creator and father, who makes us brothers and sisters, whereas it is in the nature of secularism to underrate our human interdependence. Human nature nonetheless finds a way of shining through. Woke's utopian commitments to equality and justice can never fill the 'love gap' created by secularism, not least because it uses tactics that promote hate over love.

- 'What a piece of work is a man.'

   That I cannot repeat a Shakespearean line without getting complicated over the sexist language it is perceived to contain shows how suffocating our modern society has become.

   Thank you for that monologue on the purpose of the human person. The idea that came across strongest for me was that, when all is said and done, the logic of a world without God is that 'the self' must be placed first. After all, in a godless world, on what basis could anyone else justify receiving that honour? On the other hand, a world with a Christian God doesn't diminish the importance of others, rather it elevates them to the level of brothers and sisters.

But is the selfish picture of secularism that you have painted a fair one? There are secular humanists who affirm the worth, dignity and autonomy of the individual and the right of every human being to the greatest possible freedom compatible with the rights of others. They show that they care for humanity and for future generations. They see morality to be an intrinsic part of human nature and to be based on a concern for others.

I agree that on its face the picture I have painted may appear unjust. But what I have outlined is a logical consequence of a godless approach, for it is God that gives meaning even to human nature. My argument is based on first principles, not on the actions of specific individuals. Ideas do have consequences although these may not always be manifested at the level of the individual. I readily accept that there are atheists and agnostics who show more concern for fellow human beings than some of their Christian counterparts do. But for me such comparisons provide examples, in both Christian and secularist worldviews, of persons who do not live in accordance with their professed ideals. After all, some people are critical realists and manage the fallout from their ideas pragmatically, while other people simply don't seek coherence in their lives.

The case you make for your secular humanist friends could theoretically lead to a caring society. But in practice, as society further detaches from Christianity, the humanising influence of religious thought diminishes, as can be seen for example in society's approach to human life itself. This is because secularists accept that human nature is a social construct, they over-emphasise personal autonomy and they do not see fundamental freedoms as being intrinsic to the person.

You might expect that as both Christianity and secularism value reason – which is our dominant faculty – that the outcomes of these worldviews would not diverge so widely. But it is the limitations that secularism places on reason that is its Achilles heel. Secularist reason ignores God, whereas it is the religious acceptance of God that makes the other human person fully meaningful in themselves, rather than they be seen as an extension of, or limitation on, an individual's pursuit of personal freedom. As a common father, God has made all persons his children – brothers and sisters of each other. On the other hand, in one secular model, humans are more like planets who share a solar system

– they do have limited interactions with each other, but each must respond to a desire to follow one's own preferred orbit. Planets with emotions added on, yes, but even feelings, without God, can be seen by some secularists as purely physiological responses, with no deeper reality than that of the gravitational pulls between the planets. Author and historian, Douglas Murray, who described himself as an atheist, prompted by an idea of Cardinal Ratzinger, sees great value in unbelievers living their lives as if God existed.

- You said you were a practical type – that you work from real life experience. Even if not all secularists (or indeed

Christians) are logically consistent, the consequences of this God v Godless approach must show up somewhere. Where do you see the cultural differences that you outline playing out as day-to-day realities?

- These differences are in evidence. For example, the most obvious starting point is to see how Christianity promotes the idea that we have a responsibility to look after each other, that we should see the face of Jesus Christ in the other person. Thus, charity has a deep meaning in the Christian worldview. (When this Christian aspect is missing in Christian institutions, even the secular world demands accountability.) Where the Christian message is lived fully, it helps highlight underlying human injustices in society. This in turn can have the effect of shaming the wider society into action. Universal education and hospital and healthcare systems provide numerous examples of major responses of justice which initially arose from such Christian origins.

  In modern times, the difference in religious and secular world views can be seen clearly in those institutions that serve people at the beginning and end of life. Secular societies have no problem elevating an individual's right to choose above another individual's right to life. This requires that they dismiss the possibility that the unborn child has any rights whatsoever. Such is secular, or to use a historically correct term, pagan, behaviour, and it can be traced back to long before the beginnings of Christianity. Likewise, at the end of life, the secular view is that the individual's right to choose when to die must trump any concerns that other elderly or mentally incapacitated persons could become open to undue or improper influence to end their lives prematurely. That latter outcome may not be directly intended, but it becomes an actual fruit of the secular over-focussing on personal rights. Those suffering disability may also suffer the harshness of secularism, the value of their lives being questioned in utilitarian terms, especially as they grow older, although these may find themselves legally sheltered or even supported by another facet of secularism – its allegiance to equality. That said, such a request that equality be considered in this way has not worked out well for disabled unborn children in modern secular societies.

A 1984 BBC news report of a 'biblical famine' in Ethiopia spurred musician Bob Geldof to put together a group of artists to fundraise to alleviate the suffering being caused by that widespread famine. Their song, *Do They Know Its Christmas,* became the best-selling single in UK chart history. Drawing on the humanitarian instincts of western society, its sentiments were inherently Christian:

Here's to you

Raise a glass for everyone

Spare a thought this yuletide for the deprived

If the table was turned would you survive

Here's to them

Underneath that burning sun

You ain't gotta feel guilt just selfless

Give a little help to the helpless

Do they know it's Christmas time at all?

Feed the world...

It was a call for selflessness, a message that secularism has diffi-culty in expressing.

The impact of godlessness in society is also evident in economic structures – for example, the acceptance of enormous wealth disparities – and in social structures – as for example, in the dis-mantling of the traditional family. And, as we have been discuss-ing, the decline in allegiance to the key principles underpinning democracy is also due to God having been sidelined.

- You make a strong argument for the worthwhile fruits of the Christian messages of loving God and loving our fellow humanity. But some of my friends who have little, if any, residual Christianity would generally view themselves as caring people. Where does that come from? Are they de-lusional? If secularism is so cold and uncaring as you say, what is making them immune? Why do they too not see the limitations of secularism?

- Well, their caring nature may be a Christian fruit that has been handed down to them, or they may even have imbibed it from having you as a friend. Additionally, even should it wish to, sec-ularism cannot entirely displace one's humanitarian concerns or one's natural feelings for the rest of humanity. There is an enormous human reward that comes from looking after fellow humans – and Christianity would argue, as this solidarity is part of our human makeup, that it is more fulfilling than any other thing we might do. Such personal rewards from selfless actions do not go unnoticed on the level of feelings, if experienced by your friends, even if ideologically they are secularists.

As to your friends not seeing all of secularism's limitations, the problem is partially due to the gradual way that secularism has unfolded itself. At first glance it seems reasonable to affirm 'I have no right to interfere with another person's right', but this places the focus firmly on personal rights while forgetting about responsibilities to neighbour. Additionally, if powerful voices in society push a certain secular individualistic narrative, it can be easier to go along with that rather than question the intentions behind it. Once the narrative is accepted by enough people then that becomes the culture, outside of which, as you yourself have experienced, there is anxiety. I like to think of the prevailing culture operating in a manner similar to the sun in the sky – its overwhelming light leads people to ignore the greatness of the star-filled universe that it hides from them.

In any event, going forward, in the face of secularism's emerging limitations, I am not sure the next generation will have this same excuse of naivety that is available to secularists of today.

- If secularism is so undesirable, then how has it obtained its place of dominance in western culture? Christianity was the leading worldview in the Western world for a long time. Yet, it lost its dominance. How did this come about –

is it that Christianity is out of touch with mankind's needs, and that the world has progressed better without it?

– As I said, our modern secular culture grew out of Christianity. While secularism now dominates our western societal worldview, it does not mean that Christianity has been totally displaced – it is probably truer to say that while the Christian impact has certainly diminished, it has also gone underground. The secular dominance arose in part because of the solution that was adopted to solve historical church-state tensions some centuries ago. The question at the time was how society should best balance the responsibilities of temporal rulers looking after the here and now with those of spiritual rulers who have a longer-term vision of helping us fulfil our meaning and purpose. The agreements reached in the 19th century may have left Christians with influence on society, but all real temporal power was placed in the hands of the secular state. As time progressed, religion was gradually removed from the public square. Initially it was seen as unnecessary for public life; later its views were ultimately seen as a nuisance, even if these views were only being voiced from the side-lines of society. Christianity allowed itself to be silenced, Christian individuals at times being naïve, often thinking that it was the good thing to do, in the name of pluralist thinking.

There is a strong tendency for human societies to become totalitarian. This can be seen for example when a state, suspecting any allegiances of its citizens that are independent of it, seeks to suppress these. The most recent five-year plan currently in operation in China – which now forbids young people from attending church and is gradually seeking to control Church messaging – shows how totalitarianism, once embedded, constantly seeks further controls on persons. (Similar totalitarian tendencies were on display in Western democracies during the Covid pandemic, although, for the most part, their impact was ultimately constrained by democratic checks and balances.) Yet the existence of any allegiance independent of the state, such as a religious voice, provides a strong countervailing force to the state's exercise of power over the individual. Thus, even if one did not want to hear any religious voice in the public square, a strong anti-tyranny argument can be made for the value of its persistence. Anecdotally, it would appear that modern resistance-style movements, the short-lived Canadian truckers' convoy being an example, have a disproportionate religious inspiration. And even secularists longed for the official Russian Orthodox voice to depart from supporting Putin's war in Ukraine!

I sometimes think in terms of a football metaphor when looking at how modern democracy treats religion. Originally, Christianity organised the pitch and the rules of the game. Secularism agreed but insisted that the referee, with his or her deliberative power, be on its side. Gradually, the referee lost all independence, and the rules were all interpreted in favour of secularism. Now Christians find that they are no longer wanted on the pitch.

- Well, if that is true then why has there not a reaction against this decline of religious voices? Surely no one wants to live in a cold, uncaring, secular society?

– Don't be so sure. Secularism is seen to have real advantages. Humans don't mind being selfish, as they enjoy its fruits. They incorrectly attribute Western society's wealth, driven by the success of modern science and of the marketplace, to the secular approach. (While secularists have never been shy about claiming such success for their worldview, modern societal wealth is primarily a function of scientific and technological advances, and the exercise of personal freedoms, all of which benefit from God's presence, rather than his absence. However, the modern excesses of these developments – such as unrestrained scientific experimentation, capitalist exploitation tendencies, global warming and international wealth disparities – are precisely a result of the absence of moral influences, due to God's demotion.)

Secular language – which emphasises non-interference in personal rights – deceives. It pretends it is enhancing freedom while at the same time denying public space to those who might criticise the mirage of freedom presented by its ever-increasing progressiveness (there being no limit to freedom as licence!)

I am not arguing that secular societies act only in immoral ways – these clearly do respond to genuine inequalities, by way providing services, especially to the needy or oppressed, either through the market or the state. One can readily point to very secularised communities where public services for all are of a high standard. Speaking generally across most societies, services, although now secular, were often built on what was initially provided through Christian charity – schools, hospitals and clinics, being clear examples – and that original spirit may continue to inform them.

However, other more materialistic principles do tend to lessen the quality of services over time.

For example, in countries that allow euthanasia and assisted suicide, cost factors have subsequently been used as a general argument by some to persuade people to end their lives. Palliative care budgets are reduced, thus encouraging the use of assisted suicide. Demands on health budgets lead to spending being based on materialistic considerations only. Caring professionals avoid geriatric specialities lest they be required to provide euthanasia. Doctors who are anxious to ease the burden of the dying, rather than hastening death, get gradually displaced by bean-counters who coldly propose when a person's time to move on has come.

Over time, as God gradually disappears from the public square, people forget that there is an alternative way to the secular one.

- But is it solely secularism that is the obstacle to Christianity holding its own in the world?

- No. Apart from the bad example of some Christians (a perennial aspect of fallen human nature), another factor in the demise of the religious influence on culture has been the impact of the scientific method and of the scientism that has developed from it.

The scientific method has its own inherent strength and has shown impressive explanatory and technological fruit. Science is good at describing things, with scientific theories proving themselves by their predictive powers, but science itself should be embarrassed by the over-strong case that secularism makes for it. Scientists are aware of science's limitations – it is a method, it provides a good description of the world and its workings, but in recent times scientists have become even more aware of how little is actually known. Secularism took science and sought to hitch the idea of truth solely to the wagon of science and pro-posed the scientific way of looking at the world as the only way to know the truth of things.

Secularism proposed that this scientism explains all of life, by applying the scientific method to all areas of thought such as re-ligion, philosophy and the humanities, as well as seeing the sci-entific method as the only way we should determine values. One negative consequence of this is the reductionist way secularism views truth. Philosophic and religious values – handed down as wisdom – as they are not susceptible to the evaluative measures of the natural sciences, become meaningless. Thus, for example, the value of loving another person is beyond all scientific mea-sure – over time, it reduces love to a give-and-take transactional exchange that helps secure order in society. Marriage, instead of being a total self-giving of persons, becomes transactional in nature.

I don't want to blame science for the loss of romance, but this transactional view of marriage is a far cry from how poet-song-writer Leonard Cohen expresses the importance of love (al-though he was not necessarily addressing marital love) in his *'If I Didn't Have Your Love'*:

> If the sun would lose its light
>
> And we lived an endless night

And there was nothing left

That you could feel

That's how it would be

What my life would seem to me

If I didn't have your love

To make it real.

Here, for Cohen, reality is experienced in love (and elsewhere, he acknowledges the experience of reality also in pain and in suffering). Love is the creative force in the world, or returning to Geldof, it is selflessness that solves our problems.

- I see the picture you are painting. Your complaint is with the ideology of scientism and of secularism and where these lead, rather than the persons who get caught up in their snares. Secularism, insofar as it is the fruit of scientific reasoning, is heartless – but then, what else can one expect from cold scientific logic?

But we Gen Zers now have a solution for all that: we have sought to restore its heart! We don't ignore our neighbour. No previous generation has placed such an emphasis on demanding equality and justice in society as we now do. The systemic faults of the past are being called to account by my peers. Should I not be proud of that fruit of our new secularism?

It is true that your generation is exposing some of the ideological deficiencies of secularism. Having jettisoned Christianity, it took some time for the resultant loss of Christian thinking to work its way through society. In the meantime, one could say that secularism lived off the fruits of the Christian worldview in a parasitical way until it was fully ready to go it alone.

Now, this new generation of yours is showing dissatisfaction and uneasiness with secularism's unthinking selfishness. For Gen Zers the barren meaninglessness seems intolerable, and the focus of material consumerism appears empty. Your generation sees growing inequality. It sees selfish consumerism contributing to the climate emergency. For me, all this is a sign that human nature cannot be forever suppressed. As it is part of our nature to be moral, Gen Zers are now seeking to inject secular culture with some purpose beyond the self, namely greater equality and justice across all of society. This is the morality that woke culture claims it brings.

It also brings unwelcome stuff with it that we cannot afford to ignore and will have to return to. Going back to my analogy of the football match. Secularism may have exercised undue influence on the referee to manipulate the rules to suit its objectives. However, woke culture goes much further: it claims that the original pitch had never been level, that the rulebooks need to be torn up and society needs to begin again. Though, on this occasion, the starting point must be a secular one of reinventing everything – because, as secularism teaches, there are no given truths to work with. Inevitably, this woke plan will fail if only because it doesn't have a coherent strategy beyond upending or destroying all structures. More significantly, its utopian outlook does not consider human nature's tendency to mess things up. There may be some moral purpose in woke, but it has an unreal view of society, and it has outlined no path to achieve its aim. It is driven only by hope, and its methodology, I am afraid to say, is one of hate. Rather than reconciling different groups in society it amplifies the differences between them, seeking to deny basic human dignity to what it identifies as oppressor groups.

I seem to be doing a lot of the talking! One thing has been puzzling me since you agreed to this series of conversations. Initially, you claimed that your generation had lost its very understanding of freedom. Having been so quick to accuse me of judgementalism early on, I was very surprised that you were as forthright as you were in making such a damning judgement of your own. Now that we have come around to talking about modern woke culture perhaps you would like to discuss this further.

- Yes, I must confess to some judgemental hastiness at that time. But it followed on from the logic of my generation not supporting freedom of expression. If people are not even allowed to say what they think then it is clear to me that my culture doesn't understand what freedom truly is. I will have to dwell on this some more before I permit you draw me out on it. The explanation you have provided on how different worldviews see the human person should help me clarify my ideas.

By the way, your harsh judgement on wokeism – that its method is one of hate – didn't pass unnoticed. Another provocative judgement from you, I fear! However, I do share some of your concerns. Maybe after I clarify my ideas on my culture's understanding of freedom, we can look at what hate is, because I am worried about how this term is being widely used in today's politics. Will you allow me an uninterrupted monologue so that I can string a few ideas together on how I see freedom? Some of what I will say is already clear to you, but I would like to make a fully coherent argument for your consideration.

– Absolutely. Conversations are as much about listening as they are about speaking.

I am sorry for being so blunt with you at times, but we have had so few conversations over these past few years that it is almost as if I have been ignored by you. Now, let's hear it for freedom! For the future fruitfulness of our relationship, we should be trying to be on the same side, to have some shared narrative, at least on this topic.

RAMBLIN' MAN

A monologue exploring how secularism has turned freedom into licence and how the absence of a moral heart within secularism has led to the emergence of the new virulent woke strain which, although lacking in good manners, has moral intent. Christian charity, in its display of social concern, leaves both liberal secularism and woke secularism in the shade.

Freedom from constraint is a common theme of the twentieth century philosophy. Hank Williams, one of the fathers of country music, presents that challenge on a personal level in his great tune *Ramblin' Man:*

I can settle down and be doin' just fine

'Til I hear an old train rollin' down the line

Then I hurry straight home and pack

And if I didn't go, I believe I'd blow my stack

I love you, baby

But you gotta understand

When the Lord made me

He made a ramblin' man.

The story is one of a constant tug-of-war between the protagonist's love for a woman and his need for ultimate freedom. He rejects the judgment of his peers while insisting on his need to respond to some primal urge in his personality:

Some folks might say that I'm no good

That I wouldn't settle down if I could

But when that open road starts to callin' me

There's somethin' o'er the hill that I gotta see.

Finally, when he comes to sit in judgment on himself, he insists, in a very modern self-centred way, that the world must shape itself to fit his mentality:

I love you, baby

But you gotta understand

When the Lord made me

He made a ramblin' man.

Williams' song, despite predating the revolutions of the Sixties, provides a valuable insight into how personal freedom is viewed in a secular culture.

Freedom as self-autonomy

In previous conversations we have touched upon some of what I have to say here. Modern secularism operates on the basis that things just are, that they have no purpose or meaning. We are cosmic dust that somehow gravity and biological forces have assembled into rational clumps, and that prompt us, for no obvious reason, to pursue freedom. How meaningless dust can end up being rational is a conundrum, but living with that mystery it is a small price to pay for secularism's proclaimed successes, in particular the quality of life generated in secular democratic societies over the past two centuries.

In today's secular society, the individual, somewhat like Ramblin' Man, relying on self-autonomy, weaves a path through life, maximising his or her freedoms and agreeing with others on the rules one should live by. There are no objective truths to guide these actions, other than those practical empirical truths that can be rationally worked out, with previous Christian influences having been gradually and very effectively side-lined.

Even the liberal market economy, once more family conscious, is skewed heavily in favour of each individual maximising one's own financial benefit, although the moral influence of the Christian message continues to temper it to some degree. The secular democratic state operates on the majority principle, with a winner-takes-all mentality, as can be seen in its gradual dismissal of previously Christian-inspired laws. Marriage laws, for example, now display a conviction that marriage has nothing much to offer the individual – asking as it does too great a surrender of freedom and providing little practical measurable benefit in return. Even Williams' Ramblin' Man appreciated such commitment more. Consequently, marriage does not have the lustre it once had – fewer get married, break-ups happen more easily and there are ever increasing numbers of single-person households. The progressive drift is towards equal public approval and support for any companionship arrangements involving any number of consenting adults.

Sex has come to be viewed primarily as a pleasurable experience to be enjoyed by the individual with no normative behaviours to be recommended in society. There remains one significant taboo – sex between adults and consenting (and non-consenting) children is still unacceptable. A drift towards permissiveness in this latter behaviour was arrested a generation ago when the shocking damage done to young people by paedophilia was publicised. Radical progressive proponents of sex between children and adults may publicly continue to apologise for past expressions of support for such behaviours, yet the inexorable drift towards the removal of this last taboo is still encouraged. Currently, it is assisted by calls to provide suitable pornography for children.

In the secular worldview the individual is king or queen in his or her own domain and can express himself or herself as he or she wishes; even the biological reality of sex is seen today as another social construct. Personal autonomy also extends to not feeling obliged, following pregnancy, to bring children into the world, and to being able to leave this world, with the help of the state, at the time of one's own choosing.

For secularism then, freedom is licence, which may have to suffer some limits imposed by our communitarian existence, but with the balance always weighing heavily in favour of the individual. And if managing this licence requires some degree of social schizophrenia then, like Ramblin' Man, so be it. Individual freedoms appear to be limited ultimately by the demands of good taste, as conceived by a small number of judges in court, or by what is tolerable by the majority vote in parliament. The individual in secular society can be who they want to be, whenever they want to be. Yet, despite this, Western society is witnessing an epidemic of adolescent mental health issues as well as escalating and significant numbers of celebrities, among others, overdosing or committing suicide, suggesting that this unlimited freedom is intolerable, at least for some. The father of sociology Emile Durkheim saw suicide arising as a result of society not regulating the expectations of its members, thus leaving them unclear as to their goals, with anomie setting in. Even as Finland is lauded in the World Happiness Report as the happiest country in the world, suicide rates there remain well above the European average. One third of all deaths among 15 to 24-year-olds in Finland are caused by suicide. Individuals and society require basic boundaries, some overarching canopy that points towards meaning, thus providing hope and optimism. Secularism ignores this need.

Seeking to restore a heart

The working out of secularism has led to a modern rebellion against its lack of morality. Whereas the origin of that woke rebellion may have communist-style roots, these seek to capitalise on the good nature of humankind.

Heartlessness is not a genuine mark of humanity. Secularism's absence of a true concern for others, which you earlier identified, and which is evidenced today by clear global inequalities, lies at the root of my generation's openness to the new woke secular rebellion against the 'liberal' secular model. Woke secularism shows its humanity by expressing concern for the group. It argues that freedom for groups can be best obtained by pursuing equality and overcoming injustices. Some individual freedoms secured by secularism – on the grounds of personal autonomy – may continue to have value in the woke society, but woke requires a readjustment of currently accepted freedoms to achieve equality for identified sections of society based on such differences as colour, race, sex and gender.

Destroying the roots of society

However, in establishing this new woke hierarchy of freedoms, freedom of expression has become a cropper. This freedom, if ever seen in such terms by wokeness, is viewed as secondary to the need to restore justice and equality. True woke thinking actually proposes that freedom of expression has been one the most egregious culprits in advancing the existing rotten structures in society – in allowing dominant discourses to drown out valid minority voices. Thus, it requires that this sacred cow of democracy be discarded. Incidentally, the make-up of families is also caught in the radical clean-out, the family also being a rotten structure which proposes unacceptable discourses.

Woke justice doesn't stop there. It has much more to say than that. Secularism proposed that all institutions and values are socially constructed. Its woke children now see all these human-made structures as systemically rotten – as if built with pyrite and mica – so all these institutions must be demolished to allow society to go back to the drawing board and to begin again.

Personally, I find the specific limitations on free speech maddening. These are manifested in a variety of ways such as censoring, no-platforming or politically motivated 'fact-checking', and are sometimes even exercised under the guise of hate legislation. Men are silenced because they comprise the patriarchy and promote toxic masculinity, whiteness is to be despised, and dissenters – even those of the mildest of hues – are labelled racists, bigots, genderphobes or homophobes. No media time may be given to anti-abortion fascists.

Now, it is not that these suppressive woke tendencies have not been opposed. They have, particularly in the US, with such opposition leading to the growth of what has been termed a 'parallel economy' of alternative free-speech platforms. But whither our democracies if the divisiveness often associated with politics is allowed to seep into all aspects of our lives: our entertainment, schools, sport, workplace and the home. What hurts me most is not that my personal views may not be shared by many others, but that these are not valued enough even to be allowed to be transmitted.

This new woke strain of secularism is very effective in silencing opposition but is much less so in achieving any of its identified aims. In the US for example, where the police were called out as being systemically racist, attempts at defunding or even replacing the police have resulted in increasing crime and amateurish anarchic alternatives such as autonomous police-free zones. Those for whom such actions were supposed to benefit – oppressed people of colour – become the ones most negatively impacted by this woke policy implementation.

Institutionalising intolerance

Although wokeness has arisen as a development of secularist thinking, woke restrictions on freedom of expression directly clash with secular principles of personal autonomy, or what is sometimes known as classical liberalism. In a similar manner, woke insistence on hate legislation to protect minorities clashes with secular principles of freedom. The actual methods used by woke practitioners to silence 'oppressors' – such as removal of access to social media, blackballing, demonetising on social media, deprivation of livelihood – deny other fundamental freedoms such as freedom of association, freedom of conscience and equality before the law. In a woke world, truth by its very persistence can become hate speech. One after another, real freedoms, as I have come to understand them, fall like dominoes, having lost their places in the new woke pantheon of freedoms.

Some of the methods used to address the Covid pandemic show how far along the totalitarian road that the woke culture can go. Many governments shelved fundamental freedoms, usually with the support of a substantial majority of voters, who feared the consequences of Covid for society. Some of these governments easily dispensed with fundamental freedoms of liberty and of equality before the law, without much thought as to what they were doing, even after the limited extent of the Covid threat was laid bare.

In many societies those who sought to exercise a constitutional right to assemble to protest against the Covid measures were dealt with harshly. While it is understandable that, faced with a substantial external threat, a democratic society must resort to some diminution of freedoms, what was worrying for me was how woke societies did not even acknowledge that they were exercising exceptional powers nor questioned their right to do so. At a stage during the pandemic when it was known that many people had acquired a natural immunity from the virus, some governments still decided to mandate vaccines for all, while severely restricting the personal rights and freedoms of those who had no desire to receive the vaccine, unnecessarily creating a two- tier citizenship. The ease with which some democratic societies ignored fundamental freedoms does not bode well for the future, especially when one considers a proposed WHO-sponsored international pandemic treaty (complete with penalties) which may emasculate individual governments from taking actions preferred by their own citizens. The dire threats of Canadian politicians (and the implementation of emergency legislation that froze protestors' bank accounts) to the livelihoods of ordinary frustrated citizens involved in the 2022 Freedom Convoy stand as a warning to all. Ordinary decent truckers (who, thanks to ever-present, on-street, citizen news reporters, were seen to be what they claimed to be, ordinary people who opposed vaccine mandates) were accused of holding unacceptable views, were equated with Nazis, and were policed as if they were terrorists. In the USA, following parents' protests against mandated National School Board Association's programmes, the Association requested the Department of Justice to brand ordinary parents' opposition as 'domestic terrorism.' Similarly, the ease with which hate speech laws are being implemented, laws that can define hate as including 'distasteful speech that might cause anger', point in a direction that no true freedom lover should want to go. There are some who may see this as quibbling over small inconveniences, but when one reads of how totalitarian mindsets developed in 20th-century democracies, then these complaints cannot be dismissed as pedantry. There are some in society now loosely talking about our climate 'emergency' as potentially requiring future restrictions on fundamental freedoms. One knows instinctively that something is up when politicians seek to set one group of citizens against another, falling back on majoritarian claims in exercising their power in democratic society.

I also see an enormous difference between woke societies and that experienced when one comes across some Christian 'oasis' providing services in underserved communities. What is most strikingly missing from secular and woke cultures is the communitarian view that is common to Christianity: the acknowledgement of the value of other human beings as persons, and of the rights of those who propose alternate solutions to societal problems. A secular society may have its attractions for a young, healthy individual but the indifference it shows towards interpersonal commitments makes it deadly poisonous to families, and to the old, the vulnerable and the infirm. Wokeness overlays secularism with morality by its over-riding concern for justice and equality, but it is a harsh intolerant justice, and it lacks any acceptable mechanisms for achieving worthwhile outcomes.

To my mind, giving pre-eminence to the needs of other persons, without exception, has a satisfying feel to it. Looking out for others provides a sense of purpose. When I am looking out for the basic freedoms of others, I have a sense of being freer, and being more fulfilled. It is as if investing in the lives of fellow humans makes me freer than if I were to ignore them. This is a sentiment, a feeling, which goes against that proposed by Williams' *Ramblin' Man*, and I am not sure if it can be rationally grounded. Yet I believe it points in the direction of some truth. Maybe now that I have expressed how I understand freedom, you can help me fill in some of the blanks.

GAVE ME NO FLOWERS, WISH I DIDN'T CARE

Despite the logic of secularism, humanitarian instincts run deep. It is not surprising that directing our freedom towards investing in others is what the Christian life mandates. To have a conversation on whether woke equality and justice can trump charity requires a deeper discussion of morality.

- Thank you for sharing these insights. You acknowledge using some of my concepts in your explanation. I think this is a good thing as it shows we are on similar wavelengths. Your monologue highlights the limitations you see in both secularism and woke thinking, as well as your appreciation for Christian thought.

- I should thank you for listening, as I don't often get a chance to speak my mind.

- I could suggest a good reason for that! It might have something to do with your past tendency to ignore me – but let's not go there again! Let me instead focus on your request. You feel it is the right thing to do to look out for others, rather than always centring on yourself and your own needs. You say it enhances your sense of freedom and you want me to rationally ground this desire of yours?

- Yes, please do that, bearing in mind, as I said before, that some of my non-Christian friends are also very caring people.

- Maybe I should start by saying that your conclusions are not surprising when humankind is viewed through a Christian lens. For the Christian, humanitarianism results from universal brotherhood, whereas for those atheists who see humans as the fruit of cosmic chance, it is just one of those unexplained realities. Other non-believers see it as the outcome of some cooperative idea of reciprocity built into evolutionary theory.

Human beings have an inbuilt humanitarian desire. Thus, it happens in war or conflict that the enemy is dehumanised as a first step towards overcoming any reluctance towards their destruction. In the Rwandan genocide, the Tutsi was regularly labelled as cockroaches in the preceding months. Russian propaganda persistently described the Ukrainian leadership as Nazi paedophiles. In abortion the foetus is described as a bunch of cells.

On the other hand, Christians advance humanitarianism a step further when they follow the command of Jesus Christ to love one another. They accept that love should dominate human interactions because all humans are formed in the image and likeness of God. Love helps both the lover and the loved one to grow. Love makes the lover more God-like and is a good preparation for future greatness.

For many secularists, humanitarianism is a practical way of living, deriving from a humanist outlook, even if is not rationally explainable for those who see humans as the products of chance or for those that deny the existence of a given human nature. Sometimes it is explained as an evolutionary advantage in caring for one's family. But why should it extend to strangers, and to all strangers at that? Some secularists may argue that looking out for others allows a person to expect others to look out for them, but surely it is naïve optimism to think such example to be so powerful. Secularism inevitably struggles to make sense of charity – beyond seeing it as some form of empathy or compassion – because immaterial things cannot be properly understood solely within the framework of the methods of natural science. On the other hand, it is no accident that where there is a strong Christian influence, charitable institutions flourish.

In some ways the initial intellectual error made by secularism is inexcusable. The secular mind, in seeking to understand who human beings are, first looks at the person in whom that mind resides. From there, it misses the next obvious step which would be to reflect on the reality of other existing humans who also have intellects. Instead, secularism allows the mind to move from consideration of the individual to speculating on the value of the individual's freedom, while effectively forgetting about other persons. Some 20th-century philosophers, such as Max

Sheller, absolutely reject even the initial starting point of assuming that we are first alone and then enter relationships with others. For these thinkers, practical experience shows that the consciousness of oneself as a person is always experienced within the context of being a member of a totality or community.

Christianity finds common ground with this philosophy. It looks at the human person as he or she is, a complete but inter-dependent human being. Given that interdependence is an important part of human nature, it then makes absolute sense that human satisfaction or happiness (and the freedom that seeks it) would be tied up with other persons – that investing in others enhances one's own happiness and is therefore a valid object of one's freedom. In short, human beings are made to love others, and their freedom revels in that fact. Some humanists also appreciate this dimension of mankind as one of the joys of living (without necessarily being able to explain why it might be so). Denying the reality of true inter-dependence leads one along a path of spiritual emptiness.

I hope that gives you a sufficient rational explanation as to why the very existence of other people increases the possibilities for your freedom.

- I think you have nailed it. We invest our freedom in others, for good or ill, because it is the most natural thing to do. Bond songster, Billy Eilish, well known for her presentation of the Grammy-winning, Bond-theme hit *'No Time to Die'*, is the musical star of my generation. Her dark and melancholic lyrics reflect the frustrations of our age and draw attention to modern spiritual nihilism. In her 2021 big summer hit, *Lost Cause,* she invests her love in a typical unreliable Gen Zer, with unsurprising results. She complains:

> You weren't even there that day
> I was waitin' on you
> I wondered if you aware that day was the last straw
> for me …
>
> I sent you flowers
> Did you even care?

It slowly dawns on her that any man who owes his likeability primarily to his personality or special charisma ('you think you're such an outlaw') should be easy to come by, as this requires very little effort from him

> that was way before I realized
> Someone like you would always be so easy to find.

A truer measure of the worth of a person, she reckons, is their capacity to hold down a job. She expresses her bitter realisation:

> But you got no job
>
> You ain't nothin' but a lost cause.

Then comes her damning indictment of our age as she recognises the man's inability to think about others and to put the other person first. Narcissism rules the roost!

I used to think you were shy
But maybe you just had nothing on your mind
Maybe you were thinkin' 'bout yourself all the time.

In the end comes the painful awareness that what she naively understood to be due to immaturity – which can be outgrown – turns out to be, in fact, the typical Gen Z finished product!

Thought you would've grown eventually, but you proved me wrong
You ain't nothing but a lost cause.

The loss of the Christian understanding of love as self-giving, and of the value of investing one's freedom in another person, is bound to lead to unhappiness at a personal and social level. Christians themselves are not exonerated from blame. Yet there is no doubt that Western society, while providing individuals with the highest quality of material existence ever known to humankind (admittedly at a high – or too high? – cost which is now only being acknowledged), is also delivering spiritual nihilism, which is reflected in the emptiness of people's lives. Receiving your greatest desires to your door by next day delivery should make you happy, the culture tells you – so you should not be complaining! But as Bob Geldof might say, 'Is that it?' Contradictory as it might sound, the reality is that our happiness lies in investing in others, not in ourselves.

I must also add that, in that song, *Lost Cause*, Billy Eilish does not provide a comprehensive picture of our generation. I realise I have been harsh in some of my criticisms of wokeness, yet it must be acknowledged that we Gen Zers are displaying a new flourishing of human regard for fellow man through seeking equality and justice. Surely this is as powerful as practising charity?

-   First, let me say how I see the woke contribution to society before I critique it. Many in your generation are unhappy with secularism's individualistic approach that has exacerbated economic, racial or gender disparities across the world. Your generation says that growing inequalities must be addressed and resulting injustices must now be remedied. In short, Gen Zers recognise that there are wrongs that must be put right. Once we start calling out things to be right and wrong, we move into the area of morality. So, for me to discuss woke thinking fully, I need to start calling out what is right and wrong. But I need you permission to go there, to move into the realm of judgements. For the moment, let me just say, in answer your question: addressing injustices and inequalities are good things in principle and these may coincide with charity, but do not necessarily do so. One must also look at the means used to achieve these ends.

-   Then we should talk more about morality, about exactly what things are right and what are wrong?

- Are you sure that is what you want to do? You may begin to see me making a lot of judgements. Yet, at the same time, I will try to soften any potential harshness they may contain.

- Go ahead. That time has probably arrived.

- Why so many people readily accept woke morality? I think it is a strong reaction against secularism's overemphasis on the individual, as well as against current economic disparities and other inequalities. Globalisation has led to ever-increasing wealth disparities with some individuals in the world now much richer than even many countries. Your generation has responded by waking up to the need for greater equality and justice. It is rebelling against the selfish individualism of secularist thought and is instead promoting a collectivist, group-centred justice.

  For me, such a moral awakening, while its methods may be misplaced, is practical proof of the wisdom of religious worldviews and the need for them. Humans are moral by nature. They have an inbuilt need to call out injustice and concomitant inequality. Secularism could not have expected morality to remain buried forever. The woke moral approach could be described as adding a religious dimension to secularism.

  We agreed earlier that woke actions limit personal freedoms and are undesirable for that reason. But even if there was nothing wrong with woke practices, they would still be ineffective in achieving their goals because woke theory has identified the wrong means. For example, in pursuing the business world to adopt equity and diversity programmes as a solution to inequality, it completely ignores the real problems – the enormous scale of modern wealth disparities and a meta-capitalism that appears answerable to no one. Perhaps this is one reason why some major corporates now promote woke thinking – it is a small price to pay to allow unjustified massive salary pay-outs or disproportionate profits to go unchallenged. It also provides these companies with additional levers of control over their staff.

My biggest issue with woke thinking is that it uses deeply unjust means that are diametrically opposed to Christian notions of justice – the woke answer is to seek to oppress the identified oppressors, whereas the Christian response is one of dialogue and charity.

- By now you are speaking to the converted on that final point. My culture is very woke, but I am wise enough to realise that the woke tactics are not a solution – encouraging the suppression of others is far from any notion of freedom that I share.

- Our conclusion must be that it is not enough to express a desire for just outcomes, or to have noble aspirations, if the means you use to attain your ambitions are not in themselves good.

It is strange how mankind again finds itself in a similar position as in the last century. Then it was Marxism that preached equality, and that won the hearts and minds of young revolutionary types who subsequently ended up forcing their viewpoint on others using totalitarian means. Even great minds like George Orwell had blind spots when it came to seeing the obvious evil activity of Marxist revolutionaries. Marxism too had its utopian goal, but it had no reasonable way to achieve it. Millions of lost lives later, society emerged from the darkness of communism wondering how it could have been so foolish.

While I acknowledge the worth of searching for equality and justice, we have avoided discussing what woke culture exactly means by those two terms. Just as the Marxist idea of equality is unreal – as it denies the hierarchies that are inbuilt in us as part of our human nature – such unreal determinations may also underpin woke's considerations. And if justice for woke is equivalent to equality, then woke's version of justice may also be an unreal objective. One can see the US justice system now suffering woke strains: with high-profile, individual innocence and guilt verdicts being portrayed in racial terms, with lawyers not making themselves available for unwoke causes or clients, and with many district attorneys not seeing all individuals as equal before the law. Expressed bluntly, the danger with woke is that it multiplies the problems, but it doesn't actually have real solutions to any of them – it talks a good game but when it comes to answers, in modern parlance, it is faking it.

That's worth thinking about a lot more! On coming to power in Russia Lenin threw out all structures, but even he had a plan he considered might work.

But we are now firmly threading on the previous forbidden territory of morality. So, before going further or getting more personal about this I need your formal approval. I want to remind you that (a) you regularly accused me of being judgemental and (b) you confessed that your reluctance to converse with me was not just an issue of anxiety – but that you knew what I was going to say, and you didn't was to hear any of my negative judgments of you. Due to your reluctance, I have generally sought, until now, to steer clear of speaking about right and wrong, of discussing morality on a personal level. You have asked me now to go there, so I take that to be a sign that you are ready to take any subsequent hits that may come with that.

- The short answer is yes. I do want you to go there and I am ready to address any personal embarrassments that may arise in considering moral questions. As you have wisely said, it is part of our human nature to look at the world through a moral lens. Thanks to what you described as woke morality, even secularists are now aware of that.

I do need to learn how to identify right from wrong. When you get around to talking about the tools we use to evaluate right from wrong, I suspect I may find that I am on the wrong side of the tracks on occasions. That prospect angers me. I don't know why, but it just does.

- OK, I understand that. We haven't talked directly about emotions, and anger is a key one of those. Emotions are important, so you need to understand them and appreciate their place in decision making. That is another one of secularism's mistakes: decision making isn't the cold logic it makes it out to be, as emotions have their part to play. In fact, one might argue that whereas old-fashioned secularism is cold and calculating, it is wokeness that brings emotion and feeling to the table, although it often overdoes this, as witnessed to by the behaviour of some woke warriors. This is one reason why it can be difficult to talk to woke people – their feelings create defensive barriers that are hard for others to scale.

To start, let us see where the common ground on morality might be in society by asking you a simple question: 'Is it right to kill an innocent human being?'

- No, it's not! Life is our most fundamental possession. With-out it, we cannot appreciate all the freedoms we have been talking about. Anyway, as a Christian I know that taking life is wrong – I have read about Cain and Abel.

- Good, but now try to answer the question as someone who is at home in secular society and who appreciates its secular laws.

- The answer is still no. Even if we are only formed from cos-mic dust particles, there is still a basic humanitarian idea that we should respect life. We must start somewhere. If we don't collectively respect life, then someone else might easily decide that my life should be taken next. We all have good reason to expect that life be respected by all.

- So then, as there is common ground between worldviews – we can thus affirm that it is possible to determine a standard, to say that something is right or wrong. That is what morality is.

- You sound on home ground here, so why not go the mono-logue route for me, as I suspect you will have a lot to say. And please continue to bear in mind that while I am not against the idea of there being right and wrong, I don't want you imposing anything on me that doesn't hang to-gether – there are to be no arbitrary impositions or rules – that is my bottom line!

STRANGE FRUIT

A monologue on morality, explaining how the moral code is written on our hearts. It is uncovered as we seek fulfilment, following on the wise exercise of our freedom. We need to care for human beings at least as much as we care for the planet.

Anti-religious sentiment has long sought to depose morality, to remove from society any value frameworks associated with religion. The depiction of morality as something imposed on us from without has successfully assisted in its demise. Once someone understands morality to be about being told what to do, that person finds pride blinding him or her to morality's benefits – instinctively no one wishes to have someone else's rules handed down to them, nor to have anything imposed on them from without. You confirmed this yourself in your own earlier opposition to discussing morality – first, you saw it as preaching, telling you what you should do; and second, it angered you, either for this or for some other reason.

Deaf to morality

Secular society, a society without God, is tone deaf when conversing about right and wrong. Woke warriors adopt a similar deafness when it comes to oppressor viewpoints. Even some Christians are caught up with auditory challenges around morality, partly because they have bought into the false idea that morality is the imposition of a set of rules, and often inexplicable medieval ones at that.

The secular deafness is rationally explainable. With no God, there is no objective truth, and there can there be no objective right or wrong. Fundamentally, everyone is free to do as they wish according to their own lights unless that freedom is curtailed because it interferes negatively with the freedom of others. Agreements on morality thus become essentially social conventions. Laws are formed in line with the majority view. Killing an innocent human being is wrong once that is agreed but, for secularists, in different circumstances the agreement could potentially be otherwise.

Secularists within a democratic system will usually seek to persuade the majority to enshrine their view in law, often resorting to individualist claims for freedoms, perhaps basing their arguments on personal emotional claims that some freedom or other is being denied and intimating that granting such freedoms will not damage others. Sometimes, if secular views are unable to gain majority parliamentary support, their proponents may instead seek to persuade the courts to prioritise individual rights over the common good of the society.

The fallacy of the secularists' majoritarian-style rationality is exposed when a decadent society agrees to do something that is clearly wrong – as for example in Nazi Germany – such as seeking to sterilise a racial minority within society or practising ethnic cleansing or conducting state-sponsored genocides. In such clear instances, common-sense dictates that there needs to be an appeal to a higher law, a greater justice.

In a secular society which stands so far back from its citizens as not to propose any morality, then for many, truth becomes 'my truth'. And why not? If there is no objective truth, an individual would appear to have much more right to seize the title of 'my truth' for their own outlook than someone else has in restricting them from doing so.

Evil exists

Rational reflection shows us that morality is a consequence of our free-dom, and not of rules. Jordan Petersen argues that when you witness an atrocity such as the Holocaust you immediately appreciate it to be something evil. The experience that you have (or can imagine) that is fur-thest away from that evil you can define as good. This then gives you the beginning of a scale with which to measure morality.

Singer Billy Holiday spread her own awareness of evil in the lyrics of *Strange Fruits*, a song written in the mid-1930s by a Jewish communist teacher on the unmentionable cruelty and suffering caused by racism. The stark powerful lyrics about a lynching in the American South brought silence wherever Holiday sang it. As a result, it became the last song of the set that she would sing each evening.

> Southern trees bear a strange fruit
>
> Blood on the leaves and blood at the root
>
> Black bodies swingin' in the Southern breeze
>
> Strange fruit hangin' from the poplar trees
>
> Pastoral scene of the gallant South
>
> The bulgin' eyes and the twisted mouth

Scent of magnolias sweet and fresh

Then the sudden smell of burnin' flesh.

Much like the 'Lest We Forget' of the First World War or later, the Shoah, the starkness of this song's words serves as a reminder that our past is not all that far away, just as evil is never too far from the door of human-kind. The unprovoked Russian invasion of Ukraine and the subsequent gross mistreatment of civilians is our modern-day equivalent of a base line against which evil can be measured.

It is through being free that we can set about doing what we see as 'the good'. Christian thinking embraces the common-sense perception that there is a higher law to which humans are beholden. This view overlaps with other religions that espouse the existence of an objective truth to which all humanity is bound. This truth, or the rightness or wrongness of things, is written in human nature and is discernible, using King Solomon's term, by a 'listening' heart. By responding to the requirements of this truth, people fulfil their human destiny and their nature as creat-ed human beings. It is what humankind is made for. In this, each person achieves fulfilment in the present life as well as it being the ideal prepa-ration for eternal life. Not surprisingly – due to human interdependence – such an attitude in life not only serves the individual well, but it serves the whole of society well also, a society in which all are attached by strong fraternal bonds.

Human persons are not, as secularism might have it, isolated boats on un-charted high seas exploring autonomous freedoms while seeking to max-imise their material wellbeing in the here and now. When all is going well such selfishness can be disguised by surface-level good neighbourliness among the sailors, but when the storm waves prove too much, secularism can become a case of every man for himself.

Morality innate in our nature

Right and wrong are not imposed from outside but are an innate part of this world. Morality is not the outcome of some class or group warfare, but is innate, and can be measured on any scale that has, for example, Strange Fruit at the bottom end of it. Our world is not simply a finite world of material things and experiences and events, but it is also a world of morality and meaning which enrich all lives in the here and now, not to speak of the hereafter. The laws we observe, that lead to 'rules', are not external, but internal to us as persons, reflecting the truth and reality of our created existence. There are no upper limits to our greatness but there are lower limits to which we cannot afford to sink – it is these limits that are expressed in the negative precepts of the moral law, the 'thou shalt nots' that oblige us all. Every individual's life comprises of real stories, events and happenings in the physical world, and all have moral meaning.

A moral life is not about living rules, but rather about fulfilment. To identify morality as 'rules' is to blind people to the benefits that are inextricably linked to the wise exercise of freedom. The opportunities for genuine fulfilment may be ignored in favour of short-term material or sensual gain, and therein lies what could be described as the foolish exercise of freedom.

As morality is written on our hearts then it can be uncovered by secularists just as it can be by Christians, although Christians who live a moral life coherent with their faith are better equipped to recognise and respond to it. In making distinctions in the 1940s war-torn society in which he lived, Elie Wiesel, subsequently the foremost spokesperson on the Holocaust, used a challenging categorisation for what he witnessed: 'In the place that I come from, society was composed of three simple categories: the killers, the victims, and the bystanders.' For Wiesel was concerned by indifference, and constantly warned of its danger, because he saw that 'indifference is always the friend of the enemy, for it benefits the aggressor – never his victim, whose pain is magnified when he or she feels forgotten.' For him, it was a denial of humanity:

> Of course, indifference can be tempting -- more than that, seductive. It is so much easier to look away from victims. It is so much easier to avoid such rude interruptions to our work, our dreams, our hopes. It is, after all, awkward, troublesome, to be involved in another person's pain and despair. Yet, for the person who is indifferent, his or her neighbour are of no consequence. And, therefore, their lives are meaningless. Their hidden or even visible anguish is of no interest. Indifference reduces the Other to an abstraction.

Rules facilitate freedom

In educating children it may be useful to spell out rules, rather than engage in higher order thinking that they are unable to process. In this way, they can build good habits that will later help them to appreciate and identify what is good when they are confronted with moral choices. As adulthood beckons, these rules should be pointed out for what they are, valuable signposts that seek to enhance freedom, to achieve personal fulfilment.

But what of the Judaeo-Christian commandments you ask? Are those not binding, limiting rules? This is what the great St Augustine has to say: 'The beginning of freedom is to be free from crimes... such as murder, adultery, fornication, theft, fraud, sacrilege and so forth. Once one is without these crimes (and every Christian should be without them), one begins to lift up one's head towards freedom. But this is only the beginning of freedom...'

So, to live a moral life, as it is understood by Christians, is to maximise personal freedom. The 'rules' are signposts, they do not inhibit, but rather facilitate freedom. 'The truth will set you free.'

I realise that I have spoken a lot about Christian morality without speaking directly of God. He has not been forgotten. Suffice to say for the present that he is the great genius behind this harmonious existence, and at some stage that genius must be acknowledged.

While slow to adopt a Christian morality of the person, your generation is absolutely accepting of similar moral notions when these relate to looking after the planet. Although not specifically acknowledging God, Gen Zers accept the created harmonious existence of our world; the reality of signposts, especially climate-related ones; and the inbuilt 'rules' that do not inhibit, but which ultimately facilitate our planet being as it should be. There is a clear sense that freedom allows use but not misuse. Such thinking is a small logical step from accepting the goodness of our Creator and our 'special' creation as humans. God cares for all creation, but he cares for human beings from within, through human faculties that show the right way to exercise freedom.

In reflecting on the making of judgements it is hard to have sympathy for secularists who believe they can apply scientific method to determine the morality of any action. Where do they think empirical reason could have got that power over right and wrong?

And there are also those who wish to judge the morality of an action by its consequences. Whether it is right to experiment on the human genome or to create ever-more destructive chemical and biological weapons cannot ever be weighed up against the potential immeasurable damage these may or may not do. The only practical answer that such an impoverished moral system can (and often does) arrive at is that if you can do it, then why would you not do so? As we can never tell what tomorrow might bring, then looking down the path of future consequences is to reduce momentous questions of right and wrong to the status of a lottery.

Jordan Petersen, in seeing humanity on its search for meaning, points out that we need a map, and that science in unable to point us in any direction nor provide the ethical input needed. Science can describe the terrain we pass though extremely well, but not tell us much about where we need to go.

I'LL NOT BE USED, MISLED, DECEIVED OR ABUSED

How does one align what one wishes to do with what is right to do? The answer requires an understanding of all the various actors in a person's decision-making process: intellect, will, feelings, memory, imagination and conscience, and an acknowledgement that it is the whole person who acts. The dialogue uncovers a previously unrevealed relationship between the interlocutors.

- The most helpful takeaways from that monologue were your reminders that morality is not subjective and that one cannot reasonably calculate right or wrong by seeking to predict the outcomes or consequences of any particular action.

This latter consideration is more obvious nowadays given the impacts of globalisation and the increased pace of change of society. How can anyone expect to be able to pre-judge the consequences of a careless disregard for safety measures in a virus laboratory? Or how can one evaluate how momentous a single midnight presidential tweet might be? Trying to decide whether an action is right or wrong based on its possible foreseen consequences is a fool's game in our highly inter-connected global society.

I am also glad that you have put the idea of 'my truth' to bed. If morality were to be that subjective then on what basis could you condemn any action of another person? Solely base it on a majority vote? With a 'my truth' mentality even Hitler could excuse himself. Or a racist jury could excuse a lynching mob. That is why the UN Declaration of Human Rights, which was formulated after the Second World War, chose to speak of fundamental rights deriving from our very humanity.

I can also clearly see the morality involved in interfering with freedom of expression – this freedom is not given by any state but rather it pre-exists the state; it inheres in us as a need of our nature; therefore, suppressing it is morally wrong.

I suppose the important thing for my future, if I am to be a moral person, is to seek to align what I see as best for me with what is the right thing to do. But that raises important questions. Who is it that decides what I should or should not do – is it my reason? By this I mean my complete reason and not a secular-reduced empirical reason. Or do my emotions have a part to play? I know my will commands me to act, but where does the will permission to give that command? And, what happens if I do the wrong thing?

Should I worry about that? And if I do wrong, am I then forever off the right track? Will I become even more lost in the woods than I am at present? Will that increase my levels of anxiety?

- These are valuable questions. Inherently you may have an awareness of the answers but not have the confidence to assert them. We can work our way through some of these together. The latter questions on the consequences of wrongdoing move us necessarily into deeper religious territory, as they raise questions about the link between the here-and-now and the afterlife. That perhaps could be a later conversation. So, let's see…. When you decide to do something – who decides?

- Well, that is probably the easiest of all those questions. I know there are some who will argue that there is no real freedom, that some decisions are made, for example, not by me but primarily by the sugar bacteria in my stomach responding to their microenvironment. Certainly, there may be many biological and neurological factors behind every decision, but ultimately it is I who make the decision. I decide.

- Exactly, you decide! Songwriter Paul Anka, best known for writing Sinatra's '*My Way*', has a lesser-known song in which he asserts that it is the free person who makes his own decisions.

   I'm not anyone

   No not just anyone

I have the right to lead

A life fulfilled with every need

I'm not any man

Designed to fit someone's plan

I have my own desires

Of the things a man aspires

I'll not be used

Misled, deceived or abused

No sir not me

I am free

And I'll not give away

The freedom I have is the same

To say I do I don't

I will or I won't.

You may receive signals and advice from all quarters, within and without, but it is *you* who decides.

-   But when I decide, is it my intellect that makes the decision?

-   It plays its part, but your decision and your subsequent actions belong to all of your person, not just to a part of you. When you act it is the whole of you that is acting. If you rob a shop, it is not just the legs that carry you in there and help you with your getaway that are held responsible. You, all of you, are punished by society, should you get caught!

American songwriter, John Legend, in deciding to go all in in love, sings in *All of Me*

Cards on the table, we're both showing hearts

Risking it all, though it's hard.

He does so because he realises that true romantic love is about the whole person loving the whole of the other person and is shown by each person giving themselves totally to the other:

'Cause all of me

Loves all of you

Love your curves and all your edges

All your perfect imperfections

Give your all to me

I'll give my all to you.

In all our actions it is the whole person who acts. Likewise, the whole person is involved in the decision-making process. Obviously, you mentioned the intellect as being involved. But do oth-er parts of you have any say in the decision?

- Now, I see where you are going! My emotions have some part to play. Feelings are involved, are they not? Often it is my emotions, such as anger or hatred or joy, that prompt me to act.

- Absolutely.

- I know these cannot be allowed to rule the roost. Many woke friends don't have any override systems on their emotions – they get worked up to the degree that they can-not properly reason or listen to alternative viewpoints.

Reason needs to be involved, in seeking to work things out. Reason draws on my understanding of who I am – that I am a human person who can think, that I am interconnected and dependent also on other humans. Before acting, I also reflect on previous related actions – so that must mean that my memory is also involved. If a past action of mine has had negative consequences, then I am less likely to repeat it.

- And there is also what you learn from others and not just from your personal experience – thus from history, that is, the past. That is another way that memory plays a role – it re-presents the past to you.

- And my imagination! Sometimes it initiates actions, and

then my emotions or my reason get involved. At times, imagination can be in the driving seat, drawing in all sorts of emotions that then take over, leaving my reason as a passenger on the journey.

- I think we are getting there. Recall again what Shakespeare had to say about our complexity as humans: 'what a piece of work is a man...' We are now back on familiar territory – we are thinking about the whole person being responsible.

- But we must consider other influences as not everyone is a free agent in their actions. Some of my friends have addictions, so that they may even act against their reason. For some, 'just one more pint' is wishful thinking. Others are overcome with irresistible urges to engage with gambling apps. Alternatively, other people can be frozen by fear or insecurity, with their emotions restricting their capacity to act. There are many who are unable to resist the demands of the bully, be that another person or some internal disordered passion insisting on its way. Or, as in my case, others can be so blinded by their culture that they don't always see the obvious wrong.

- Well, I think we can agree that any single action is laden with complexity – it is a wonder we ever get around to acting! Now, suppose you want to make a here-and-now decision – how do you pull all those influences together to ensure you do the right thing?

- I think about the action, and I try to take all the factors we discussed into account: reason, emotions, memory, imagination. I seek to ensure that my reason is not bullied especially by my emotions, then I decide – my will decides – and after that I follow through with the action.

- Fine, but in all that complexity at what stage will you come to a decision that what you are doing is the right thing? It is not enough to be able to do something, to have the capacity to do it. The real test of your humanity is your response to the question as to whether this is the right thing to do. Does this action further you as a person? How will you decide that?

- Very good point!

- That is where I come in.

- Say that again. What do you mean – that is where you come in? Who are you in all this process?

- I am the one whom you have accused of always seeking to have an agenda, of being judgemental, of moralising. With your cooperation these past few weeks I have managed to gently dismantle the barriers you have erected against me, undoubtedly constructed initially with the connivance of your culture. I have not done any of this surreptitiously. I have always sought your approval. I have had to apologise to you on multiple occasions so that we kept our channels of communication open and that you could continue talking to me. An independent onlooker might say that I should have called you to task on those occasions –

that I was a coward in not standing up to your constant prevarication. But no, it wasn't cowardice on my part. I gave you the space to allow you build up your trust in me. I wanted you to realise that I just don't randomly set out to shock you or shame you or set you on a guilt trip. As you now know, you, as a person who makes decisions, are much more than your emotions. You are a bundle comprising all the things we have just identified: your reason, your imagination, your memory, your emotions. But also, me. You must include me in the bundle!

My name is conscience. Consider me as part of your intelligence. I apply universal knowledge of what is good to any specific situation here and now, and express a judgment about what the right conduct is. In short, my job is to help you to choose the good. I do that by presenting it to you in as attractive a way as is possible. In the ideal circumstance you listen and are guided by my voice. But ultimately it is you, the whole you, who decides, then your will commands your body to carry out the action.

I have an additional role which is to admonish you when you do wrong, so that perhaps my correction will help you pay more attention to me on the next occasion.

I want to be your friend. I want you to trust me. I want you to converse with me as we have been doing these past few weeks. I want you to do the right thing. It is for this reason that others have described me as the echo of God's voice within you.

- What? This is all too much for me to take in. That's who you are? After all this time, now you have come clean. Yes, we have happily talked together. But you have also niggled at and nagged me. And now, you are effectively confessing to being the one responsible for inducing shame and for facilitating my guilt trips. After all that, you want me to trust you and to continue to be a friend to you?

- Hold up there now! I have tried to do my best. You are a free agent, as you have always been. It has always been within your control to involve me or not in your life. In recent years, I have knocked hard on your door, incessantly, trying to get through to you. Wrapped up in your culture and all its external trappings, you have seldom heard me. You opened the door wider some weeks ago, thus these pleasant discussions, which I hope we can continue.

- I am guilty as charged, entranced by the bright lights and loud music of my surroundings I must admit. But I feel anger growing within me. I am not sure why? Do I feel you have deceived me? Maybe it would be prudent to postpone this conversation and resume it at another time when my calm has been restored?

- Whatever? You are the boss. I have 'given my all to you' in recent days, and you have reciprocated in giving 'your all to me'. There has been no holding back, no deception. Things have been going very well between us. I would hate that all our recent progress might be undermined by an unnecessary and avoidable, emotionally fuelled row. So, a breather would be in order.

WE TRIPPED LIGHTLY ALONG THE LEDGE

A conversation about the characteristics of conscience: how it aligns itself with objective truth, the battles it has with the emotions, and how its important work can be wrongly presented as a limitation rather than an enhancement of freedom. All the talk about morality begins to spill over into a discussion of the religious understanding of the person.

- I think our last conversation was a real shock to you. You were deeply puzzled by the nature of our relationship. I hope that by now that you have fully restored your equilibrium.

- I am certainly on the path to recovery. We did the right thing by suspending our conversation as I must admit to being very angry at the time. Here was I revealing to you all my innermost thoughts, only to find out that you already know me as well as I know myself. All that said, the circumstance was completely of my own creation, choosing as I did to blind myself to certain realities, to indulge in self-deception. I gave you the impression on the last occasion that I was completely puzzled by our relationship, whereas it would be truer to say that when we first engaged in dialogue it was more convenient for me to forget who you were. Speaking with you as one might do with a friend was easier than facing up to who you really were, so that's why I chose that route.

- I understand the temptation to avoid internal dialogue – it is much easier to go with the flow of the culture and not to think too much about making decisions for ourselves. But, in the eternal words of Socrates, 'an unexamined life is not worth living.' Facing up to conscience should not be such a big deal. Conscience may not be the flavour of our age, but it still has a respectable pedigree. Eminem gives it good profile, although he goes on to make bad use of Dr Dre as a conscience figure in *Guilty Conscience*. Zerocalcare in his comic strips shows a healthier respect for conscience which he is not shy to depict as an unmistakable, giant armadillo. Not everyone understands the extent of conscience's role, but at least conscience is out there, visible, and has some limited respectability in your culture. I should also point out, because I know it troubles you, that it is incorrect for you to say that I know everything about you. Only God knows you in your fullness as a person.

- Fair enough, but you know all the important stuff, the moral stuff. You know all that badness that is within me, the awful things that I have done, the shameful things. You must know all that, don't you?

- That's true. I am a witness to any unfaithfulness or badness of yours. But I also have witnessed all the noble struggles you have undertaken, the battles you have engaged in, the valiant efforts you have made to do the right thing. I know all the true goodness that you have displayed as well. Our friend, Aleksandr Solzhenitsyn, rightly observed that 'the line dividing between good and evil cuts through the heart of every human being. And who is willing to destroy a piece of his own heart?' Thus, humans will always have a tendency towards badness within them, so why be upset by that? It is not these tendencies that determine us, but the decisions we make. For the world-renowned psychologist Jordan Peterson, the challenge each person faces in life is to understand the Auschwitz prison guard that is within them, to recognise one's capacity for evil and to identify what can be done to become a better person.

- But the bad overshadows the good in me? It must.

- Well, that judgement is away above my pay grade. All I can say is that when I came knocking in recent weeks you opened up to me. That is a sign that you are moving that division line in your heart to one side, pushing down on the badness and enlarging your capacity for the good. Anyone ready to have the conversations we have had is already on the right path. Also, on the positive side, you now realise that you can have complete trust in me. I am only here to help you to do the good, so in everything I say I have your good in mind. I have no self-interest colouring my view, I say what needs to be said come what may, and my guidance is absolutely reliable.

- Our conversations have convinced me of your credentials. As my inner voice these past few weeks you have been a great help to me in analysing my cultural surroundings and guiding me in my responses. But tell me what you mean by absolute reliability.

- It means simply that if you follow my guidance then you can be sure that you are doing the right thing, that which is true.

- But I thought truth and right and wrong were objective. But by listening to an inner voice… is that not subjective? How does that square up?

- That is good logic, but I would like you to follow through more carefully on it. You are correct in saying that truth is objective — it is outside you, you yourself don't make something to be true. My job, when you are facing any specific situation, is to apply the universal knowledge of the good and to then express a judgment on the proposed course of action. I don't pull my view out of a hat, nor do I allow feelings and emotions the prerogative of independently determining the criteria of good and evil. My job is to seek out objective truth and to present it to you. If I do my job correctly then you can be sure that following my advice is absolutely reliable.

- But how do you know what objective truth is? How do you know what the right thing to do is?

- Well, much of that depends on you. You, that is your reason, must supply me with the right resources so that I am informed. Then, I will do my homework and if I am sure an action is good and I tell you to act, then, despite any other pressure you come under from, say, your feelings, you are bound to follow my advice – if you wish to do the good.

- Exactly what sort of homework do you do?

- It is not as if you are a blank slate. Right and wrong are written on your heart. You also have available your full untrammelled reason, your imagination, your emotions and your memory, plus any good guidance that you can find. I pull these sources together and advise you as to whether the action is right or wrong.

- But surely you are not infallible – you must make mistakes? What if that action turns out subsequently to be a wrong one? What if things are not quite as you perceived them to be, and I end up doing evil?

- If you carry out a wrong action following on my advice – what is commonly called acting with a certain (but erroneous) conscience – then no blame accrues to you. However, if it emerges that you have short-changed me, that you have not provided me with all the necessary background or information, or if I am deficient in my knowledge because of your carelessness, then I can be mistaken in the advice I give you. In that case, you are to blame, not necessarily for the wrong action but for undermining me and keeping me in the dark, causing me to give you misleading advice. Additionally, any persistence in bad behaviour by you over time can deaden my influence on you, leading you to pay no attention to me whatsoever. In such cases I can end up playing very little part in your decision making. Remember last year? I know I was deliberately shut out by you. That is why it is helpful for you to develop good habits – these leave you more disposed towards listening to me.

- I prefer not to review my past, thank you. Everyone nowadays says that they follow their conscience. I have seen people do what I would regard as fundamentally evil acts and excusing these, based on their conscience. How can their conscience on such occasions be absolutely reliable, as you are claiming?

- Certainly, there are people whose conscience is misinformed – they may wish to do the right thing, but they are misguided. There are many others who, despite their claims of following conscience, do not know what conscience is and are thus very unlikely to be following it. For these people, they understand conscience to be an extension of their will – it is another way of them saying, 'I want to do this, so I will do this, and I don't have to listen to the objections of others.' On other occasions, what some people call conscience is a fancy word for their dominant emotion – 'I feel like doing it. I feel this is the right thing to do, so it is the right thing to do.' I can wager you that such people have never experienced rich conversations as the ones we are having. It is worth remembering that claiming a right to exercise freedom of conscience or to be allowed follow one's conscience arises precisely because one's conscience also has duties, that is, specifically to seek and to follow the truth. As such, a proper claim of conscience can never legitimately be a claim for selfish autonomy.

Christians strongly uphold the rights of conscience, and the right to conscientious objection, that is, not to be forced to do anything that might go against one's fundamental beliefs. Secularists on the other hand often deny this right, arguing that it is a special claim by Christians (primarily) for a concession in secular society. This denial of conscientious objection by secularists has recently come to the fore in the medical arena where, in some jurisdictions, a person's claim to an abortion or to end their own life is prioritised over any doctor's conscientious right not to play any part in such actions. Under this logic, conscientious objection is labelled as 'refusal of care'.

The 2,500-year-old Hippocratic Oath taken by doctors reads:

> I will apply dietetic measures for the benefit of the sick according to my ability and judgment; I will keep them from harm and injustice.

> I will neither give a deadly drug to anybody who asked for it, nor will I make a suggestion to this effect. Similarly, I will not give to a woman an abortive remedy. In purity and holiness I will guard my life and my art.

Secularism, having turned the purpose of medicine on its head by first allowing doctors to kill patients under certain circumstances, now resists any claims of conscientious objection, arguing for example, that no one is forced to be a medical professional – it is a voluntary choice. The ugly totalitarian logic of secularism is clear. Many people in society would have a serious moral issue with being involved in the killing of another human being. Yet the strong secularist view, as witnessed in Canada and in some Australian states for example, is that society ought not to countenance conscientious objection in any profession, including medicine. Such people view medicine as a service industry in which patients are entitled to receive uniform service delivery from health care professionals. The proposed secularist solution for people with a conscience is for them to stay away from medicine as a career. Where this secularist logic becomes mainstream, then, within a short period of time, in the name of personal autonomy, secularism first turns medicine into a killer profession and subsequently denies the right of persons who believe in the Hippocratic Oath to even enter the profession.

Currently, it is religious thinking that is the most forthright defender of fundamental individual freedoms. But here I am again, wandering – this time into areas of rights. Maybe later when we are better prepared, we can look at rights in more detail.

- I would like then to take the opportunity to bring the discussion back to me and to my feelings. I know you may not like me constantly bringing this up, but it is important for me. In our last conversation you revealed your identity. We then suspended that exchange because I sensed I was getting angry – although at the time I could not identify the cause of it. This has also happened to me in the past, so I really want to get to the bottom of it now. I think Shakespeare's *Richard III* adequately describes my frustration when he says:

> ... O coward conscience, how dost thou afflict me!...
> My conscience hath a thousand several tongues,
> And every tongue brings in a several tale,
> And every tale condemns me for a villain.

I get angry thinking of how much you make me suffer. Why do you make me feel uncomfortable, or guilty or ashamed of some of my actions? That is what makes me resent you. This is why we have had breakdowns in communication in the past. But you know that! You have driven me at times into a deep sense of remorse. You know how miserable I can be in these situations, but you don't relent. That does not square with you being a trustworthy friend.

- It is not my job to make you feel good. It is my job to help you to do the right thing, one consequence of which is that you are more likely to feel good, although not necessarily when I am chastising you.

- OK. But that doesn't explain why you should make me feel rotten about myself?

- When your body is in pain, you want to be free of the suffering, but you are also aware that the pain is alerting you to some underlying threat that may need attention. Shame and guilt could be described as the emotional equivalents of pain – they indicate that something wrong is happening. They are often initiated by me to get you to reflect on your actions, to consider what you are doing, when you are not on the path of the good. These may not get you to change your mind, as often the die has been cast by then, but they do tell you that something is not right.

As these are emotions, I don't fully control them. Sometimes your guilt or shame may be misplaced – that's not always my doing. In general, when you have successfully balanced all the vested interests in any intended action, and you have gone ahead, acting contrary to my advice, then that is the backdrop against which you experience guilt or shame. My job is to try to maximise the correct side of the Solzhenitsyn dividing-line that runs through your heart, to maximise the good you do – it will often hurt, but it is worthwhile.

-   I take that point. But the shame and guilt usually follow on after I have behaved stupidly. What is the use of that? Surely that is too late to be of help to me, so why inflict it?

-   Because there is always a next time! You will then have those negative experiences to look back on as part of your future guidance. This emotional pain is also meant to purify you, to get you to reflect. But it does not have an automatic or mechanical corrective effect, as if it did, that would be removing your freedom from you. Nonetheless, the pain should help you to focus on fundamental questions, to review your relationship with good and evil, with right and wrong. In the past you have been generally responsive to that restorative effect, which is part of the reason why you have been open to these conversations.

- Now that I am being totally honest with you, I must admit I have always been very impatient with your moralising, even when I knew you were right. I have felt you constantly encroaching on my freedoms. I understand better your intention now – you don't want me to waste my freedom in pursuing any wrong paths. I am beginning to appreciate that the right path isn't necessarily the most attractive path – that my emotions and my imagination can be more skilful than you in making their options attractive to me. Because your offer, although the right one, is often less appealing, I am inclined to resent or dislike what you recommend – which I now appreciate you are only making for my good (otherwise, you would not be presenting it to me).

- Patrick Kavanagh's great love song *On Raglan Road* captures the inner challenge often presented by conscience. In his case 'he had loved not as I should a creature made of clay' and knew it could only end in tears, yet he continued on:

  > On Grafton Street in November, we tripped lightly along the ledge
  >
  > Of the deep ravine where can be seen the worth of passion's pledge.

  This is how Kavanagh acknowledges the conscience he is ready to ignore:

  > On Raglan Road on an autumn day I saw her first and knew

That her dark hair would weave a snare that I might one day rue;

I saw the danger, yet I passed along the enchanted way,

And I said, let grief be a fallen leaf at the dawning of the day.

- I suppose I should be more grateful for your pointing out the dangers to me, rather than complaining about your interventions! It can at difficult at times to see the good or, like Kavanagh experienced, to do it once it has been seen!

- The Book of Genesis explains the source of our moral malaise as the original sin of our first parents, a corruption of human nature. The good can be hard for a person to do. Not only that, but if a person develops a habit of avoiding the good, that further adds to the difficulty of ever doing it. Often when you ignore me and choose to do something wrong, you get attached to that wrongdoing, making it harder for you to show any further interest in what I have to say. If I could draw a comparison with the scientific worldview that tells us that entropy is always increasing in our universe, that it is moving towards an ever-greater state of disorder, then I would say that your moral state of disorder increases with wrongdoing. You may provide yourself with 'good' reasons, but this is often a sign of you running away – that you are afraid of hearing what is truly good, that you fear that doing that good will cause you more pain than you are ready to endure.

- That's true. My emotions or passions can be very strong at times. I can get wrapped up in myself and become the centre of my universe. When I am in that form, you, frankly, can be a nuisance. I now accept that this is partly why this series of conversations has taken so long to happen. I am sorry for my past rudeness.

-   You are right about the emotions, and they need to be kept in check. They can become slavedrivers, if one is not careful, much like addictions are. Now that you are aware that it is my mission to help you then perhaps you might listen more to me. Talk can be liberating, and, as I have previously quoted from scripture, it is truth that sets us free. Negative feelings and emotions can be educational moments if you are ready to learn from them.

-   I think I am now more open to your judgements which I realise can only be a good thing. This may not be the time, but I would like to know more about the corruption of human nature that you have mentioned, this dividing line in the heart. Can you explain it more? How can something that happened at the beginning of mankind be experienced by me today? Is it a gene thing or something?

-   When discussing the woke worldview I described it as having a utopian, idealistic view of humanity. I did so because it does not show any understanding of mankind's fatal weakness — that although we may wish to do the good, we do not always succeed in following through. Consequently, inequality and injustice and many other wrongs are permanent features of humanity and will always need to be tackled.

This fundamental weakness is described in the Book of Genesis as the sin of Adam that has been passed on to us through the generations. One way to understand how that might happen is to consider the fact that humans are fundamentally relational creatures where the threads of relationships have been damaged.

For us, everything is relational: we come from the womb of another person, we are nurtured by others, we grow in the company of others, and we cannot essentially live without others. For many modern philosophers the experience of consciousness is always within the context of being a member of a community.

Adam's action damaged these interconnecting threads of humanity. First, by trying to be like God, he destroyed his relationship with God. It could no longer be a creature-Creator relationship as he had sought to become like the Creator. Adam also destroyed his capacity for human relationships as well, because by wanting to be like God he was essentially seeking to be in dominion over other human beings. Now, if you consider all humans as being networked with each other across all of time, then Adam, at the beginning, has introduced damage right across that network. Relationship bonds, all modelled on Adam's damaged bonds, are forever impaired.

Humankind does not have within itself the power to repair these bonds. From the moment humans come into this world, our actual and potential relationship capacity with others is all damaged, almost as if Adam had a damaged 'relationship-gene.' As a result, we cannot know or understand what proper relationships with one another – nor indeed with God – should look like, because Adam's action tainted every single relationship, and that damage touches every subsequent relationship. Not only that, but we are continually compounding the damage ourselves by acting out our own inappropriate understanding of relationships.

Now, if for tainted relationship I use the term 'original sin', and for additional damage I use 'personal sin', and for relationship I understand the word 'love', then this picture may make more sense to you.

- Now we certainly are on religious territory because you are talking about sin. Over the past months I noticed that anytime we got close to a religious theme you tended to slide away from it. I also observed that you have often pulled back from criticising wokeness outright. I want to assure you that as a Catholic Christian I am not afraid of having such conversations. I am saying so in case you believe that the influence of secular wokeness has created some hostility to Catholicism within me. I am also ready to listen to a full evaluation of wokeness – you cannot hurt my feelings in that regard. And if I think you are unjust in your criticism, I will let you know.

- No, I didn't think you were lost to woke. I am aware of your allegiance to your Christian faith or, to be frank and honest, I must call it your partial allegiance. But I do 'slide away' as you say. This is because many people see religion in terms of dos and don'ts, of rules that must be followed, and I wanted you to move intellectually beyond that. That cultural image of Catholicism has provided many a person with excuses not to think too much about morality. Yes, religion does present us with the Ten Commandments. These are more properly viewed as signposts, rather than rules. More importantly, as a Christian you are a follower of the person Jesus Christ, not a keeper of rules. This path is often described as a path of love, and true love is not about being bound by rules. Signposts are helpful in guiding us on the path through this life, leading us to the next. Your fundamental objective should be that of following the example of Jesus Christ, making that journey easier. I accept that we may need to discuss religion in more depth at some stage.

- Allow me one more question on religion, now, please. The more I talk to you the more aware I become of the mistakes I have made and of the many cul de sacs I have discovered along my journey. These mistakes are burdensome. Am I doomed to carry this weight of error with me through life?

-   I really don't want to talk to you about your personal sin, that is, the damage you have done to yourself, to others and to your relationship with God by your wayward actions, unless you are sure you want to discuss it. But to your question as to whether you are doomed to carry these burdens. The short answer is no. Remorse helps a person to self-correct, provided the person is open to that. You have shown you are open to it by and large, so that is a good starting position to be in. Also, your religion reassures you that Christ died for your sins. Therefore, He has created a path for you that leads back to him. Your intellect should have made known that path to you – it is through the sacraments, especially penance, that allows you to begin again. Once you use the sacraments, you can see their benefit. My best advice to you now is to inform yourself better on the fundamentals of your faith and then address sin head on. It is not just this life that should concern you, as you need to have a firm eye set on the afterlife.

    Maybe this is now another opportunity for me to complement you once again on your openness. It has allowed us to move forward – together as one, me alongside you, helping you put each next step in the right place. Perhaps going forward, you can think of me as your moral compass or your best adviser on your journey? All in all, however, I don't want to be seen as a giant yellow armadillo.

-   I appreciate your discretion in not wanting to talk more about sin with someone who has been slow to acknowledge his sins. I am getting there, so who knows what the future will bring? In the meantime, I would like us to continue our discussion on freedoms – as to which ones are important and which are not. I raise this because someone I respect insisted that I use the personal pronouns that he preferred for himself. I am happy to call him by the name he now uses, but I think this pronouns expectation is a step too far. Is there any order or limits to freedoms?

- Yes, I agree that this conversation has become too personal – who ever wants to talk about their own sin? You deserve a breather. I think it would be good to reflect on freedoms, what these are and how they work together, as this does help a person understand what it means to be fully a person and, more fundamentally, a creature of a loving God.

- Before we leave this topic of conscience, I need you to guide me. How can I explain you to my friends? How can they begin to understand the idea of an 'inner voice' within? They may have experience of their own inner voice, I may explain to them what it is, but forgive me if I say so, it is all going to sound like a made-up explanation, especially as many of them are sceptical about God's existence in the first place.

- I see your dilemma, one which is caused by living in an unbelieving culture. Maybe I could draw a parallel for you. Many talk nowadays about identity and finding one's identity. People often find their identity within a group. Group identity becomes more important for Gen Zers who are lonelier than previous generations. Delayed family formation, more broken families and much smaller family sizes all contribute to young people searching for a sense of belonging outside family. On the left of the political spectrum, identity could be found in some intersectional group, or on the right it might be some patriotic or nationalist expression.

There are two levels on which we could look at that search for identity. On the social level, a group may gather around some idea, something that they identify with, but which is outside of themselves. For example, however vaguely it may be defined, there is something called 'being Irish' with which people identify. Then on an individual level, an inner search goes on within the person to find something that would indicate alignment with that outside reality. Thus, for example, if a grandparent was Irish, or the person lived in Ireland, or the person loved to speak the Irish language – these are all inner realities that allow the person to align themselves with the outer reality, thus confirming their identity as 'Irish'. This alignment brings fulfilment. Thus, identity is something from outside but there is also an inner dimension that seeks to map onto that outer reality.

With issues of truth and morality there is a similar outer and inner reality. The outer reality is that there is an objective truth, which sometimes it can be hard to define in its fullness. There is also a right thing to do in any circumstance. The inner reality is conscience – which exists and seeks to align the inner understanding of what is right with that outer truth, so that this alignment can be used to guide one's actions. In this way the person is fulfilled.

As you can see, not only is conscience easily explainable in your modern culture, but it can also be a way of demonstrating that we are creatures made by a loving God. If all that fails, you can introduce them to Zerocalcare's giant yellow armadillo, which is a good example of an 'inner voice' at large!

NOTHING MATTERS WHEN YOU ARE FREE

There is a natural hierarchy of freedoms that derives from our human nature and our responsibilities to each other. As woke culture seeks to undermine these freedoms, it is not advisable for good people to stand by as onlookers.

- It is amazing how far these conversations can wander. Some weeks ago, we were talking about freedom before we looked at morality and how it impacts upon freedom. You then revealed to me who you were, and like the good adviser that you are, you gave me time and space to digest that information. You did say that we would go back to our conversation about freedom as it would help me appreciate fully who I am as a person. I wish to do so because I see freedoms slowly slipping away from my generation without so much as a whimper. I interpret that famous saying, possibly by Rosseau, "man is born free, but he is everywhere in chains" as a declaration that our desire for freedom is something innate, part of who we are, yet despite that, many seem ready to demurely accept impositions on their freedoms. This may be understandable to those who consider us to be random bundles of pre-determined atoms. But for the rest of us, freedom is a driving force – we want to be free. Or do we just want some types of freedom but not others?

- Perhaps a better way to put that is that our freedom is a searching, knocking on doors, seeking that which will fully satisfy us. Only in achieving this ultimate good will freedom be maximally satisfied.

There are those who reduce freedom to licence. Kris Kristofferson echoed such a vision of freedom in *'Me and Bobby McGee'*. 'Freedom is just another word for nothing left to lose', he sings, a self-centred readiness to 'trade all my tomorrows for one single yesterday.' On the other hand, there is the freedom that Pete St John's hero in *'The Fields of Athenry'* sought to win for his family as he risked his own freedom in stealing 'Trevelyan's corn, so the young might see the morn'. The sacrifice of that father is heard on the wind:

> By a lonely prison wall
>
> I heard a young man calling
>
> 'Nothing matters, Mary, when you're free
>
> Against the famine and the crown
>
> I rebelled, they cut me down
>
> Now you must raise our child with dignity.'

- Freedom, the realising of our own human will, undoubtedly reaches its highest form when a person freely giving themselves for another, just as shown by that young man. But is there any specific type of freedom that is fundamental, that is head and shoulders over the others, that everyone should have, that we should be recognising in society today? Or have all freedoms the same status? Is there an order or ranking of freedoms? If so, then how is it determined? People claim freedoms all the time – they say they have this right or that right. Very often these are empty claims and seem to have no basis other than someone is asserting them, somewhat like my friend and the use of pronouns.

- If you don't mind, I will avoid discussing rights for the present and will focus on freedoms instead. As to a hierarchy of freedoms, I am sure you know yourself what the most fundamental freedom is?

- Given that we have discussed it, then yes, I do. The freedom to be able to live – to live one's life must be the most basic freedom there is. If my life is taken from me, I cannot experience freedom in any way whatever, at least not in this world. If I am dead, then all further conversation on worldly freedom is rendered superfluous.

- True. Now consider the reality of your circumstance as a purposeful human being sharing the planet with other humans who are equally valued in the eyes of the Creator. What would you regard as your next fundamental freedom?

- As my greatness lies in thinking my own thoughts and using my reason, then anything allowing me to reflect on my relationships with my Creator and with other humans would certainly be up there. As would my freedom not just to think freely but to be able to follow through and do what I think to be the right thing. Doing the wrong thing is of no help to me, rather it sends me backwards on my path.

- It is part of your nature to be inscrutable to other individuals – they cannot tell what you are thinking. Your individuality is displayed in that opaqueness, suggesting that all freedoms connected with your individual nature and your capacity to reveal it to others, should you wish to do so, must be important, otherwise you are unable to properly communicate. What you have just outlined is freedom of belief, of worship and of conscience – all slightly different aspects of the same idea. No one has the right to force themselves inside your head, to tell you what you should think, or to force you to act against any of your fundamental beliefs. And you have the right to share these beliefs.

- OK, I am still with you. Anyone who respects the personal dignity of the individual person would acknowledge all that you have said. Although in the circumstances where the individual as individual does not count, and where only the collective matters – as for example in Marxism – then that freedom will not be honoured. I am now wondering about woke thinking – it is all about membership of groups and one's viewpoint only being that of the group, so it too has a clear problem with that aspect of freedom.

- It has a problem with all of these freedoms, as we will see, but let's not get distracted yet with wokeness. Let's keep this discussion as broad as possible. We are doing well. What would be next on your list of freedoms?

- I don't think it is a distraction. Freedom to think a certain way is linked to freedom of action. For example, woke thinking says I must speak or act only in accord with the oppressed group to which I belong – this is effectively interfering with my freedom of conscience. If I know it is wrong to carry out an action that woke thinking insists must be done as member of an identified oppressed group (for example, requiring that I censor others), and woke society tries to force or shame me into carrying it out, that can't be right.

- True, but the reason I do not want to focus on wokeness itself is because it is not only woke thinking that disrespects freedom of conscience. It has often been the way of secularism to seek to impose its worldview. It's a sort of a totalitarianism that cannot brook alternatives. For example, some liberal secular societies insist that doctors must refer patients for abortion if the patient wishes it, even if these medics do not regard abortion as being healthcare or do not consider it not to be in the best interests of the patient. Also, in some countries, Christian organisations such as adoption agencies have been forced to close down because they would only process heterosexual couples as adoptive parents, as they believed that a child had a right to a father and a mother. And we saw similar tendencies earlier in speaking about euthanasia. No attempt is made by secular society to facilitate properly grounded conscientious objection, because secularism resists addressing any claims to objective truth. Anyway, back to the list of freedoms....

– OK, I take your point. Another freedom that needs to be respected is my capacity to interact with others. If I cannot interact freely then I will never be able to reach a common story with others on how we should live together, or how we should share our planet. I have already expressed my frustrations about limitations in modern society in this regard – that there are people who would deny me my freedom to express myself. I also shouldn't forget about dealing with God or the freedom to worship, as people have sought to worship together since the dawn of time.

– This is good reasoning – you are looking at human nature and seeing what it tells you. Worship is important to us. Paradoxically, on one level it reflects an innate awareness of our nothingness, but on another level, it highlights our singular importance and our togetherness. One could argue that freedom of expression is a precondition for all freedoms, because without it our interconnectedness is emptied of meaning. And what you describe as interaction also includes freedom of assembly – again, this is a freedom that precedes the state, it inheres in you, and the state may only propose restrictions in matters of great import which are for the good of all.

Another thing I like about your reasoning is that you are seeing freedoms associated with the responsibilities that you have as an individual person and towards others. Your freedom of worship derives from your duty to your Creator, your communitarian freedoms arise because of your duties to others and to the planet we share, and that we must pass on to future generations.

One of the first duties of the state is to respect the fundamental rights that we have outlined here, otherwise it is depriving you of things that are innately yours, things that no majority has a right to take from you.

- When I started criticising woke thinking because it elevates the group over the individual, you cut me off. Am I right in suspecting that you were seeking to soften your criticism of woke warriors?

- I am sorry if I gave you that impression. At the time I simply did not want to lose our focus on the wider considerations of freedom. Now that we have considered freedom as comprehended in the Christian worldview we can address how others — especially woke thinkers — diverge from that outlook.

Simply expressed, woke thinking says that it wants justice and equality. It also states that all institutions and societal structures are systemically faulty, and these therefore must be dismantled. According to the woke understanding of the world, all the freedoms we have outlined come from oppressor worldviews, which have facilitated their development, so these freedoms must also be thrown into the dustbin to allow us to begin again. The question then of how wokeness interprets these fundamental freedoms is irrelevant, as it is intent on dismantling all of them. Wokeness seems to think that thousands of years of human development can be ignored, and that our minds can easily begin again in working out everything from scratch.

Thus far I have tip-toed around woke, conscious of your sensitivities. It is worth recalling how a famous American social activist, Dorothy Day, began an article in the 1930s on communism. She said: 'It is when the Communists are good that they are dangerous.' Woke is similarly dangerous because in demanding justice it is superficially attractive to the Christian mind. But, as I have shown you, there are also many faults with woke ideas, not least, for example, that woke responses are more emotionally driven than they are rational, and that wokeness has no workable solutions in its push towards utopia. However, its greatest fault lies in its complete blindness to our human nature, something on which Christianity has a sensible grasp. Woke thinking seems to posit that mankind can live up to any ideals it sets for itself, whereas history shows that we never have. We are constrained by our mortality; we always slipping backwards in delivering upon our ideals. For humans, utopias have never existed. Christianity explains this weakness best when it presents us with the idea of original sin: human decline is inevitable, but we should constantly seek to begin again, working within the constraints of our given nature.

- That is a top-down way of looking at woke thinking, but is it true? Surely, if wokeness was so far off course, people would disregard it as a passing fad. But that is not what is happening – a whole generation of people are showing that they buy into woke thinking!

- Oscar Wilde once said that 'a map of the world that does not include "utopia" is not worth glancing at, for it leaves out the one country at which humanity is always landing.' Our modern society, which has a poor understanding of history and of religion, can be very naïve in what it expects of humanity. It seems unable to see through this woke utopian foolishness.

Democratic society has developed a range of checks and balances to inform and enlighten its citizens including an independent media, competing political parties, a separation of powers within the state, and a variety of cultural and religious voices. Currently, these institutions appear to be all failing society, partly due to a form of institutional capture that initially started in third-level colleges a generation ago. Woke ideas that were generated on campuses at that time have filtered down throughout society and are neutering all of secular democracy's checks and balances.

Secularism now finds it has nothing to fall back on, due to its denial of objective realities, thus allowing for the woke capture of secular democracy, leading in turn to a creeping totalitarianism. Secularism has no truths to replace the ones it has gradually abandoned, nothing that might stop the march of woke ideas, a worldview that can be viewed as secularism with a conscience. Additionally, in insisting on the silencing of opponents, woke culture does not allow space for opposition voices to be heard, and in this way, it secures a cult-like grip on its adherents. Cults succeed by cutting off their adherents from alternative viewpoints. You are witnessing this regularly among your woke friends who refuse to engage in debate and who expect that you accept their views as true on face value, without discussion.

An additional strength of woke culture is that it harnesses extreme emotions of disgust, hate and intolerance towards those who oppose it or its ambitions – this misuse of emotion is another cult-like method of indoctrination. Applying extremist labels is one such favoured method of marginalising the opposition – everyone from Canadian truckers seeking to preserve their livelihoods to American parents concerned about school curricula to Polish patriots are labelled as fellow travellers of the Nazis. So, if your generation buys woke thinking it will be primarily due to the inability of secular democracy to protect itself, and because the correcting effects of the Christian worldview have not been applied.

- I have spoken to you often enough about my unease with woke. But we live in democratic society. If people freely choose to be woke, then who am I to resist that?

- After all our talk about freedom, you ask me that question? You are free to pursue the good for yourself and for others. If you want the good to be preserved for the future, then you need to play your part in that. That is the way democratic society works – you simply cannot presume that it will follow a correct course, that democracy will always be there. You will need to actively seek to persuade others what exactly the good is, if you want them to enjoy it. If you don't to that, then the miserable consequences of a woke utopian outlook become inevitable. As Elie Wiesel reminded us, indifference is not an answer: bystanders are those who turn their back on morality.

Over 150 years ago, the political philosopher John Stuart Mill likewise warned us: 'Let not anyone pacify his conscience by the delusion that he can do no harm if he takes no part and forms no opinion. Bad men need nothing more to compass their ends, than that good men should look on and do nothing. He is not a good man who, without a protest, allows wrong to be committed in his name, and with the means which he helps to supply, because he will not trouble himself to use his mind on the subject.'

Defending freedom of expression, freedom of association, freedom of conscience is also everyone's business. Freedom did not come easily around *The Fields of Athenry*

Against the famine and the crown

I rebelled, they cut me down.

Why should the battle for freedom be easy at any time? Be clear that it is a genuine, full-blooded battle! Ultimately the method of woke is to respect no freedoms – it only understands power. It will stop at nothing to undermine any institution, because it sees no value in any of them. Similar to a hurricane gathering intensity, other power-hungry ideologies feed the woke storm unless principles of freedom are firmly upheld. Such intensification is in evidence in US legal circles presently in an attempt to prevent the overturning of the 1970s Rowe v Wade abortion ruling. An unseemly demonising of judges, the description of the Court in the New York Times as an instrument of oppression, demands to fill ('pack') the Supreme Court with additional partisan judges, complaints about the undemocratic nature of courts, and the unprecedented leaking of ongoing court deliberations would all appear to be attempts, under the cloak of woke's distrust of institutions, to misuse power to achieve a particular end.

A healthy dose of the Christian message permeating your society could help awaken people from their woke slumber. You have a part to play in that. The successful promotion of a morality of respecting Mother Nature should include human nature. Preserving natural habitats can include human ecology.

Now that I am proposing your duty to you, perhaps it is time to talk about free will. Each person is free so that they can willingly seek the good. Unless you actively seek the good, then you are wasting the gift of freedom.

I COULD HAVE BEEN SOMEONE

Many things conspire to diminish free will, not least our abandonment of personal responsibility and our own hiding behind our culture. Limitations imposed on personal freedoms must be proportionate, with any relevant laws devised in a climate of freedom and built on truth.

- I was puzzled by your suggestion that we talk about free will. Is this not old ground? I understand free will as the choices we make for ourselves, the actions we decide to do, without others imposing their will on us. These may be good or evil actions, but I am correctly exercising my freedom when I am choosing what is truly best for me.

- That sounds good to me. But there is more to explore. What would you say about addicts? Are they free?

- Well, freedom seems to diminish enormously when you put a slot machine in front of a gambling addict, or when an alcoholic has access to a free bar. Theoretically, both are free, but I would be much freer than either of them in those circumstances.

- Does that mean that they are not responsible for the outcome of any of their resulting stupidities?

- Again, based on what you have already said to me, the alcoholic's most blameworthy action might have been to enter the pub, rather than any stupidity that followed on afterwards. He knew that if he walked in there that there was a strong possibility that he would lose control, so that decision was much more consequential than if it had been me who had walked into the pub for a pint. He is responsible for all his subsequent actions.

In any event, as individuals, we should be slow to blame or judge others. Yet society has no alternative but to do so at times. The unwholesome characters in The Pogues' *Fairy Tale of New York* are down on their luck and suffering judgement under the law. Ending up in prison (the 'drunk tank') over Christmas, one of the lovers reflects on lost love. You cannot fault his declared starting place, his dreams, and his investing in his loved one:

> I could have been someone
>
> Well so could anyone
>
> You took my dreams from me
>
> When I first found you
>
> I kept them with me babe
>
> I put them with my own

Can't make it all alone

I've built my dreams around you.

But somewhere along the way everything fell apart. You could argue from the lyrics that they each let the other down, but perhaps the surrounding society may also have some responsibility for their predicament. Undoubtedly there is a harshness about secular society in its inability to reach out to those in need, or address their needs – a sense of it being no country for old men or for those carrying the baggage of their failures:

They've got cars big as bars

They've got rivers of gold

But the wind goes right through you

It's no place for the old.

Despite the harsh realities of life and all the unpleasant-ness associated with failure, the lyrics manage to include a hopeful note:

So happy Christmas

I love you baby

I can see a better time

When all our dreams come true.

Sometimes when blame is properly attributed, it provides an opportunity for reflection and reconciliation and strengthens a desire to begin again.

- Are your woke warrior friends free?

- That is a good question, and one which has been exercising my mind since our last discussion. On the one hand, the answer is clearly yes. There is no one compelling them to be obnoxious to those whom they regard as forming the oppressor class. Yet at the same time I feel like I am dealing with people caught up in a cult. Their emotions have clouded their reason to the degree that they are unable to reflect rationally on their worldview. They cannot undo their wokeness. It would appear that once rationality diminishes then so too does freedom. Even if they wished to talk to oppressors, their worldview prohibits them from engaging with any conflicting voices. So, they are in a self-made prison. This prompts me to say that they are not free.

- My initial inclination is to agree with you but, on examining their circumstances more fully, my conclusion is different. They are not automatons; they have minds – and mostly college-educated ones at that – so there must be culpability for their actions. Our nature is communitarian, and they are going against that by their exclusion of others, albeit other groups. Their consciences must be alerting them to that almost puritanical wrongdoing, even if they are trapped by their worldview. So, they are culpable for their actions. It is important that you rattle the prison bars of your woke friends as often as is necessary to waken them up to reality.

It is not just woke people who create prisons for themselves. Many people brought up in a secularist culture never bring their minds around to analysing their own moral behaviour. They think to themselves that they are not doing too badly, especially when they compare themselves with the worst examples of life among those around them. They hide behind dogmatic statements like 'evolution is right' or 'religion has been proven wrong' or 'nothing is true', and they affirm that they have nothing new to learn. Or they resort to quoting specific bible passages seeking to prove to themselves that the Christian God is obviously cruel or anti-women, or pro-suicide or anti-gay, as if a single sentence taken out of context could properly catch the depth and richness of the Christian message. In such ways they absolve themselves of any notion of moral responsibility for their actions.

- This brings back to my mind a very early conversation we had about culture. As our culture provides security against people's anxieties, many are reluctant to look beyond it. When people see something happening that challenges the culture, they are quick to condemn the action without thinking – as if pleading with protagonists not to rock the boat! We must also acknowledge there is the natural comfort provided by hiding among the crowd which must be reckoned with. Yet freedom as an individual gift is wasted if all it is used for is to seek the security of the crowd.

- So, even though people today talk a lot about free will, they are less willing to properly exercise it. No one who truly appreciates the value of freedom should allow themselves to become captured by their culture. The progress of cultures through the ages shows that there is something underpinning every culture, that is, our human nature. This provides a way to measure each culture and can help ensure that the person is not imprisoned by the defects of that culture. There should be no hiding behind the culture – free will is proper to each person.

Personal dignity is measurable to the degree that we live in accord with the truth of our being. Undoubtedly, there were Aztecs who, recognising it as natural wrong-doing, stood against the practise of child sacrifice in their culture – they may not have survived long as a result. The penalties for standing up for truth against the evils in our present culture – even allowing for wokeist behaviours – are seldom as fatal.

You have a role to play in helping the people around you to exercise free will. For its full use people need to be educated in morality, as well as being able to speak freely. Free communication between people is a path to education. To be denied such input when it could be available is a form of coercion. When woke thinking or social media platforms suppress alternative viewpoints – often because these are socially or politically inconvenient to the mainstream (although sometimes they may contain untruths) – then they are complicit in that coercion.

- But there must be limits? Not everything on social media platforms is 'education.' A person can't just say anything. For example, surely racist remarks cannot be tolerated in a free society.

- Of course, a person can't just say anything, and as you say we should not tolerate racism or any denigration of people. But a full answer to your question requires that we drill down more into the details. For example, it is always reasonable that a person who makes objectively racist remarks be appropriately chastised to help him correct his ways and to ensure his ill-manner is not contagious. Thus, he might be banned from the football grounds where the remarks were made or have his social media platform access reduced or cancelled. But if the measure that has determined the charge of racism is a poorly judged one, or if the claims of racism against him are solely politically motivated, or if the actions taken lack balance, then such procedures may be unreasonable. Disproportionate actions can potentially undermine the impact of other more genuine efforts to combat racism, and so become counterproductive.

Due to our endless capacities to misuse freedom, and working under the influence of Christian principles, Western societies use the rule of law to ensure that all citizens receive equal treatment and that the exercise of power in society is not arbitrary. In turn, the development of good law requires the existence of freedom of expression within society. Thus, we start by accepting the principles of freedom of expression and of equal treatment and seek to resolve the problems of abuse downstream from there.

- I can appreciate that for just laws to be formulated further freedoms are needed, namely people need access to education and access to truthful news. Unfortunately, our media have substantially lost our trust. Somewhere along the line, due to political and commercial reasons, the commitment to truth in the news has been significantly diluted among mainstream and legacy media. The line between propaganda and truth has become so blurred that it is much harder for my generation to get things right. And if we are making law based on untruths, the resulting law is much more likely to be unjust. When some US Supreme Court justices showed themselves to be patently ignorant of key facts (as evidenced in a major public hearing in 2022 on Covid vaccine mandates), facts normally garnered from mainstream media, the enormity of the danger of an unreliable media was brought home to all.

- As we established for the individual, society also needs to operate by the same fundamental principle – that is, 'the truth will set you free'.

Therefore, your ability to fully exercise your freedom and your free will depends also on others being able to exercise their freedoms properly – a mutual inter-dependence. This should not surprise us given how much in practise we depend on each other for all our needs. Paraphrasing a great intellectual, we are a being 'from others', 'with others' and 'for others' – that is a truth that will never change.

We may never get co-existence right, but that should not stop us from being ambitious and constantly working together to seek improvement:

I can see a better time

When all our dreams come true.

Chapter 16 Hate

WHEN HATRED WITH HIS PACKAGE COMES

Woke methodology is underpinned by the destructive revolutionary tactic of stoking hatred due to difference. Redefining hate and using legislation to combat it, apart from restricting freedoms, may contribute to undermining the battle against true hatemongers.

- My culture speaks a lot about hate. It is a word widely used in society today, whereas its antonym, love, has gone underground. Or at least the true meaning of love has been lost among many counterfeits. Is that a sign that the Christian message no longer resonates as it should?

- Love never disappears, and it is its presence that helps keep hate at bay. Towards the end of the 20th century, songwriter Leonard Cohen vanished from public view to live the life of a Buddhist monk for about five years. The impact of his monastic experience was evident in his *Ten New Songs* album on his re-emergence again into 'Boogie Street', as he called his busy public existence. In one track, *'You Have Loved Enough,'* he acknowledges the power of love over hate:

That I am not the one who loves

It's love that seizes me

When hatred with his package comes

You forbid delivery

I recently mentioned hate to you when I declared that the methodology of woke culture was one of hate. You bristled at that, so perhaps that is the best place to start.

In the early years of communism in Russia, there was a move by the revolutionary government to amalgamate all farms, thus reducing the power and wealth of prosperous farmers and accruing that power to the state, through setting up farming collectives under state control. This policy of forced consolidation of individual peasant households into collective farms began by setting farmers against each other. The state turned less successful farmers against more successful ones by accusing the latter of exploiting the labour of others to achieve their prosperity. The less successful farmers were then more amenable to join collectives, and to support the confiscation of the land from the richer farmers in the name of justice. In short, by fomenting jealousies, hatred was stoked, and the collectivisation process gathered apace. The policy not only caused a drastic reduction in farming production but led to the deaths of millions of peasants who resisted the forced collectivisation, and to a famine that killed many millions more.

A similar method is used by woke society today to advance its belief system. When I use the word 'hate' in describing woke techniques I am referring to the enmity directed towards the person holding an offending view, combined with actions intended to bring about the person's downfall. This woke approach is not surprising, given the Marxist roots of the ideology. Members of so-called oppressor groups are demonised in many ways. They may be censored or shouted down, suffer violence to themselves or to their property or even lose their livelihoods. Their viewpoint is systematically denied space in the public square. These actions are justified in the name of the greater good of justice.

These expressions of hatred towards others creates newly oppressed groups who may then respond in a manner similar to the treatment they have experienced, thus setting off a cycle of hatred within society. It is much like picking at a scab on a body that is trying to heal. Society has many evident wounds, the legacies of human nature and of history, and continually seeking to make these bleed will never advance the healing.

Woke media play their part in selectively amplifying unhelpful tensions. I am not proposing that differences should be covered up, but the error oftentimes lies in the media's lack of proportion. A news station that addresses race issues by only covering the late-night racist stupidities of a small group of drunken louts obviously does not exercise the correct balance.

Imposing a group narrative on society and fomenting divisions between such groups is a recipe for stoking division. It is a return to outdated tribal instincts of a distant past. The initial mistake lies in the reductionism of encouraging humans to see themselves through one aspect of their identity, such as gender, race or colour. This creates opportunities to exploit differences by amplifying them.

Antagonism between groups in society can be further unwittingly aggravated by restorative policies. To undo an identified initial oppression, wokeness demands positive discrimination methods. This causes the state to provide preferential treatment to one group over another, likely creating a new discrimination. Thus, a tax benefit or grant support or health benefit may be given to one group in society and not to another. A newly discriminated-against person, believing that he or she personally has done no wrong, may react negatively to the new discrimination through an increasing dislike for what he or she could view as a newly emerging oppressor class.

The problem does not lie in positive discrimination per se, although state actors must be careful in establishing the necessity for such a policy and seek consensus before implementing it. The main problem lies in setting one group against another in society. Initially, the so-called oppressor group is demonised, and then its members, individually or collectively, are penalised. This is followed by the punished group seeing the injustice in this action and reacting to it by demonising the initiating group in return. Thus, a tit-for-tat cycle commences with no knowing where it could stop. Destructive political systems can quickly build up around such divisiveness.

Another noticeable reaction to woke is the stirring of nationalism: the woke left promotes tribalism and the reactionary right promotes national fervour to counteract it. The latter action is an attempt to seek solace and security in the idea of the nation, an expression of hope that national structures can keep the emerging woke 'tribes' from warring with eawch other. Unfortunately, this defensive nationalist reaction can also become accompanied by an anti-migrant sentiment, or used as cover by it, thus leading to the emergence of further us-them groupings in modern pluralist societies, where the international free-flow of people has become a constant. An inclusive, open nationalist sentiment may be a helpful antidote to woke, but not the exclusivist kind which can turn out to be woke tribalism writ larger.

To return to your question as to the decline in the Christian message of love. The cycles of hatred we witness today are certainly fuelled by a decline in religious sentiment and a lack of Christian respect for the other person. Secularism has an individualistic selfish streak that, when transferred by woke culture to the group, leads to the trampling on the innate rights of other individuals (or indeed other groups).

- I accept your analysis of the tensions that woke culture is generating throughout society. Take, for example, the Netherlands, a very secular country and one of the early European countries where the political tensions that now characterise woke thinking manifested themselves. At the turn of the century the political disagreements were primarily around migration policy. Now, today, everything has become political. A recent debate on nitrogen use, which would have been a technical one thirty years ago, now becomes a matter of national pride for Dutch farmers. Clear, overlapping political divisions on many issues are evident. The huge correspondence that exists among these convictions suggests a deep cultural divide. Political positions on Europe, on climate, on food policy and on immigration often align with lifestyle preferences, apparently dividing society into those in favour of social order and tradition on one side, and those in favour of diversity and change on the other. The division also breaks down along lines of levels of education rather than on economic positions within society, much as it does as between the 'deplorables' versus the college-educated elites in the US, or between the Canadian Freedom Convoy truckers versus the federal political establishment supporters.

But it is unfair to land all the blame on woke thinking. Right-wing nationalist feeling predates the woke effort. Many young people see Western capitalist systems as doing nothing to positively address the migration crisis, growing wealth disparities or ongoing planetary destruction. Thus, if real change is to come about, everyone supporting the status quo must be seen as the enemy. Woke thinking simply aligns dispossessed groups in a common cause.

You must also try to understand the woke individual's mindset. As you pointed out to me recently, there are some people who believe that words can create reality. In expressing their own viewpoints, oppressors are seen to be restricting the otherwise perceived unlimited freedom of others, and are denying the possibility of many good things happening. Insisting, for example, on the reality of biology over gender is seen as a fundamental denial of the freedom of those oppressed others who believe in the fluidity of gender norms and relations. Exclusion, cancellation and detestation of oppressors who deny this freedom are seen as the only possible effective responses.

Yet many who hold a woke viewpoint claim to be more reasonable than those above. Some will deny there is a cancel culture in operation at all and see it more as a much-needed, call-out culture, although if that were true a whole range of conservative voices would not now be depending on fringe media for their living. Nor would Substack have become a prestigious platform on which top international journalists like Bari Weiss and Glen Greenwald are forced to ply their trade. There are others who simply see cancel culture as a way to reduce harm while resenting the woke label being applied to them. They say they just wish to reduce hate, and deny they are oversensitive. They affirm that privilege is blinding people to existing oppression.

- I am not trying to blame woke people. I am seeking to explain the harm they are doing. In attempting to repair the damage caused by privilege they propose replacing one set of privileges with another. To remove what they view as hatred caused by oppression they promote hate towards the oppressor. They polarise rather than seek common ground for unity.

Reflecting on what you have said about The Netherlands, I cannot but believe that the absence of religious thinking, and consequently of morality, has a major part to play in the polarisation that has developed there. The Christian worldview readily highlights the wrongs in untrammelled capitalism, planetary destruction and misplaced nationalism, but rather than angrily throwing everything away it encourages proper dialogue between all sectors of society. Rather than suggest that we begin all over again without having a worked-out pathway, it proposes we continue to build using all the tried and tested freedoms that form the basis for democratic peace. It is an approach based on respect for the other (even one who might be regarded as an enemy), borne out of Christian charity. It is intolerance for the sin, never for the sinner.

- It is strange that at a time of relatively greater tolerance within Western society we see hate legislation cropping up everywhere. Even though it is not clear that there has been any significant increase in racism across Western society, there has been a greater focus on it, partly due to increasing migration, and this has resulted in many more incidents been reported. In the US, the advent of avowedly Marxist organisations like Black Lives Matter (BLM) has not only drawn attention to existing racism but has contributed to increasing it. Woke culture unfortunately then attributes every observable societal fault to racism.

In response then to real racism and to what one might term the manufactured BLM kind, 'hate' legislation has been developed. But such legislation, growing out of a lack of appreciation of foundational rights, often pitches a new right not to be offended against the right of free expression, giving greater significance to the former. According to woke culture, words can be violence, so individuals or groups expressing (legitimately held) views contrary to those of protected groups should suffer legal persecution. Thus, the danger arises in the creation of a two-tier society where everyone is no longer equal before the law. Those in protected groups are preferentially treated and can react to perceived offences by bringing the law down upon the offender. Unsurprisingly, religious viewpoints that can differ from the dominant secular narrative become targets of the totalitarian mindset of secularist groups. There have been many examples of people, including religious leaders, being charged or jailed for expressing views or carrying out actions not aligned to the dominant narrative.

In England, hate speech as a criminal offence relates to it being directly connected to another crime. If an assault is carried out, and it has been proven to be motivated by hate, then that becomes an additional aggravating matter in the prosecution of the assault crime. In England, unlike what is proposed for Ireland, it is not a crime to say what could be categorised as hateful things, unless the words used can be deemed as incitement to hatred. However English law is now also under review.

By classifying every potential or perceived misdemeanour as 'hate', the category of hate becomes devalued or possibly destroyed. In recent times, scientific papers that have made factual claims about the difference between male and female bodies have been factchecked under the guise of hate speech. Some people expressing traditional gender viewpoints have been deplatformed. Classifying an opinion that may be viewed by some as upsetting or distasteful alongside the downright vile and genuinely hate-filled may allow the true sowers of hate to escape the judgment they should receive, while robbing their victims of the appropriate protection they deserve.

Society is now moving rapidly in the direction of intolerance, in the silencing of contrarian voices, because, as we agreed earlier, it has lost the true understanding of freedom of expression.

- A strong example of this can be witnessed in Canada, regarded as one of the world's premier liberal societies. An anti-racism bill making its way through the provincial parliament in Ontario, known as Bill 67, seeks to embed critical theory within the education system. Critical theory is the postmodern Marxist idea that underpins woke culture. It denies the ideas of a free sovereign individual and free expression, seeing such ideas of freedom as the primary cause of racism and other oppressions. It accepts the principle that harm can be subjectively determined and that anyone feeling victimised is justified in claiming harm. Such leg-

islation essentially accepts that hate is in the eye of the beholder: generating a sure formula for silencing all opponents of woke
thinking.

We need less talk of hate and more talk about respecting differences in democratic society through engagement with each other. One of the great benefits of the Christian worldview is that it
understands freedom and it has transmitted that understanding
down to the present day, informing our democratic societies. As
the Christian influence diminishes, so too does society's understanding of freedom. No matter how political societies develop,
every Christian can nonetheless personally live up to, and respond
to Leonard Cohen's admonishment and

> When hatred with his package comes
>
> You forbid delivery.

The loss of understanding of freedom is mirrored in our society's
diminishing understanding of what human rights are.

- There are so many contradictions now in our world.
  Until recently the liberal secular world seemed to be
  declaring everything as a right. On the other hand,
  our secular woke culture now wishes that many fundamental freedoms be curtailed for certain groups of
  people. So, what are and what are not human rights?

- To date, I have avoided using the language of rights in our conversations because of the disputed nature of what rights are. The
  time is probably right now to go there and to explore how rights
  and freedoms should relate to each other.

WON'T YOU HELP TO SING THESE SONGS OF FREEDOM?

Freedom brings rights and responsibilities in equal measure. Only by having a proper hierarchy of freedoms and an emphasis on responsibilities can we stop human rights deteriorating into claims of personal autonomy.

- I think I understand why you postponed this conversation about rights for so long. Now that I am more committed to ideas of interdependence, I suspect you believe I am ready to have this discussion. But first let me say how my generation understands rights. Rights today are freedoms that a person claims, and that other persons should not infringe. Is that a true interpretation?

- That is certainly how many in your generation see it, but it is a very partial viewpoint. To make a claim for something does not establish that there is a right to it – at best, it should be considered as a request that the matter be studied.

Rights are downstream from freedom. Seeing rights as claims, as you have just described them, is more of a secularist way of looking at things, whereas tying rights to responsibilities, because of our interdependence, is in keeping with a religious or Christian outlook on freedom, and more in keeping with how the original declaration on human rights was perceived.

The religious view is that if you have a freedom, then you can claim an associated right to exercise it. But just as freedoms are seldom unencumbered, so it is with rights. Thus, it is important that when we talk about rights, we also talk about associated responsibilities. For example, you have a right to free assembly because you have a duty to worship with others and to help shape society with others. You don't have it so that you can organise riots, although you may choose to take that course of action.

On the other hand, secularism doesn't see rights in the same way. First, by having no allegiance to anything pre-existing the person, secularism begins with the idea of individual freedom and idealises the freedom to the degree that it is seen as licence; then secularism seeks to ensure (via rights claims) that this freedom is unencumbered as much as possible by any claims made by others.

On a societal level, secularism has no qualms in using emotional responses to difficult, individual circumstances in order to advance personal rights claims, at the expense of the common good of society. If it is for my personal good, then secularism argues it is also for the common good. Despite the wisdom contained in the phrase 'hard cases making for bad law', secularism will often present individual hard cases as a method of claiming a right, in the knowledge that compassion for the individual can easily blind the public to their wider responsibilities towards society. Anti-life laws are often advanced using such methods. Secularism sees no fault in this approach as, for it, individual personal freedoms trump societal claims.

A free society is built on the notion that you can express yourself freely. Since the way you express yourself can impact negatively on other people's freedoms, it is not surprising that some restrictions will arise. For example, free expression does not include a right to tell lies about others. You may still decide to do so, but society will likely punish you for it. You need to exercise your freedom morally, cognisant of what is right and wrong. In the ideal circumstance you should exercise your freedom to achieve the good, or in an ideal society the law should not restrict your freedom to do what is good.

- What you are saying is that I am free and so is everyone else, but that exercising my freedom must necessarily involve respecting the freedoms of others as well as my own.

- Exactly. So, you can talk about your right to exercise your freedoms, but you must understand the responsibilities that accompany those freedoms.

- I can see now where it is useful in society to have an agreed hierarchy of freedoms. If my right to free expression is high up the ladder of freedoms, then someone else's claim or right not to be upset by what I have to say cannot necessarily trump it. This doesn't mean I should go around deliberately upsetting people, but it accepts that this may happen – that this is a price society must pay for the good of free expression. The woke thinking that says people should be silenced for expressing views that disrespect others is a travesty of free expression. Obviously, the state can seek through its laws to limit my right to free expression (for example libel or slander laws), but it should not do so arbitrarily, or in a partisan way, and it must always bear in mind the basis of my right and the common good of society, and not just the needs of those who might be upset at my viewpoint. A clear example of an acceptable limitation of free expression might be the so-called 'Don't Say Gay' law in Florida (actually known as the Parental Rights in Education Act). This law requires that classroom instruction by school personnel or third parties on sexual orientation or gender identity may not occur in kindergarten through grade 3 (up to 8 years of age) or in a manner that is not age appropriate or developmentally appropriate. Its legitimacy lies in an understandable acceptance that children and explicit sexual ideas do not mix, a fear of parents that vulnerable children might be subject to inappropriate gender or anti-family propaganda, and a heightened awareness of attempts by ideologues to turn schools into re-education camps. In this case, parents' educational rights clearly trump any claim of teachers' freedom of expression – especially where the audiences are captive – or any attempts at indoctrination. Equally, one would expect that young children would also be protected from explicitly violent material, including gruesome material related to abortion or to war.

- You are correct in saying that there are some freedoms that are more fundamental than others. This was not a controversial idea when the UN Declaration of Human Rights was established in 1949. That Declaration was a response to Nazi war actions that, although allowed under German law, were adjudged as crimes against humanity that any right-thinking person should not commit. This was an implicit acknowledgement that there was a law of nature written in our hearts, that we could therefore know, by which we could distinguish good from evil, and against which we should not resile.

As secular liberalism has evolved in the direction of greater personal autonomy so too has the interpretation of many personal rights dimensions in UN treaties. Secularism insists that all we have is our personal autonomy, our empirical methods of knowing truth, and our freedom. It diminishes the importance of our human nature, our mutual interconnectedness, and our responsibilities towards each other. By not recognising objective truth, secularism leaves personal freedom drifting in the direction of licence, to the degree that the only restrictions on personal freedom become ones imposed by emotions rather than reason, that is, those imposed by good taste. Secularism has no issue in calling out black to be white, if that is what those in power – as they seek to maximise personal freedom – decide it to be. Secularism's strong focus on personal autonomy is also why it is weak on solidarity and does not do charity well.

- Yes, I have seen this in recent times. Who would have thought that the most natural human differences between woman and man, biological differences, might be a matter for debate? Once the truth of human nature is denied there is no obvious lower limit to falsehood. As society increasingly prioritises personal autonomy under the guise of rights legislation, it becomes very hard for many good people to continue to be enthusiastic about what are called human rights.

However, the basic truths of human rights should not be obscured. Such rights exist, they are universal, and all persons are subjects of these rights. These are unchanging values common to all of humanity. Everyone has them; they cannot be lost or misplaced, nor can they be legitimately denied or removed. Unfortunately, the human rights vocabulary has been shown to be vulnerable to misuse in promoting the desires of self-serving ideologies and in redrawing human nature. The use of the term 'reproductive rights' to cover up for the denial of the rights of unborn children is one such egregious example. In this climate, it is not clear to me that human rights can continue to retain their prestige, thus denying the vulnerable in society what was once a valuable defence weapon. What we have to remember is that human rights are universal, but these no longer coincide with those rights promoted by secularised Western society: narrow cultural impositions now seek to replace universal rights.

In his famous *Redemption Song,* in which he denounces slavery and oppression, Bob Marley shows that he has no time for those who don't stand up for freedom.

> How long shall they kill our prophets
>
> While we stand aside and look?

He encourages us to join the fight for freedoms, yet the modern Western dilution of human rights makes it difficult to identify what are the important battles. Marley wants us to join in, but no longer can we distinguish easily between universal freedoms and the claims of ideologies.

> Won't you help to sing
>
> These songs of freedom?
>
> 'Cause all I ever have
>
> Redemption songs.

While millions worldwide continue to be unable to sing their own Redemption Songs due to a lack of fundamental freedoms such as freedom of assembly, of expression and of religion, the Western-influenced UN agencies concern themselves primarily with marginal ideologies. Viewing the unfolding disaster in Afghanistan following the 2021 US departure, one cannot overlook the fact that Afghan society appears to have risked the Taliban's return rather than supporting the continual imposition of Western cultural ideologies.

One area where a significant cultural rights' clash is evident internationally is the present push for a right to end one's life at a time of one's choosing. A majority in many Western societies appear open to accepting euthanasia and assisted suicide, despite the impact this would have on vulnerable minorities. But can this be truly a right?

- That is a good example of the ideological clash over rights. Logically, it is clear that a right to die cannot co-exist with a right to life. To exercise a right to die one person must be given a power over the life of another, thus potentially undermining everyone's right to life. Or for a person expressing suicidal thoughts, which often can be transitory, a right to die implies that others do not have a right to interfere.

Some argue that in such circumstances the power of killing is only being given over certain lives, that is those who wish to forfeit their lives under particular conditions, but in practise those limitations cannot be guaranteed. For example, a right to die directly empowers a strong anti-life sentiment among some medics at the expense of weaker patients. Studies show that many patients who choose assisted suicide do so as they fear (or are led to fear) they are a burden on others. The old and vulnerable may make demands on others, but to declare these as burdensome is a rejection of the natural cycle of life. Everyone is a burden on others at some time or another. Fear and duress are easily generated among older persons – in these circumstances they cannot be said to be exercising genuine freedom.

Even if one were to accept that someone had a right to die at the time of their choosing, this would necessitate the involvement of others, as to vindicate the right would ordinarily require the help of others. Thus, an onus is placed on unspecified others to be available as killers. In some countries where there is a right to euthanasia, nursing homes that were not ready to grant it to patients have had to close, and doctors unwilling to conduct euthanasia have been suspended. In short, a right granted to a few quickly becomes a new unwanted duty on the many.

So, by using reason and reflecting on the nature of man, and on right and wrong, one can come to an understanding of what human freedoms are and what are true rights and the responsibilities related to them. As the modern interpretation of rights moves inexorably in the direction of claims, and freedom is seen as licence, one must be even more insistent on the need to anchor rights with responsibilities. Often this can help a person to distinguish between what is a genuine right and what is merely a claim.

It may be difficult, and others may often 'stand aside', but you have a duty to fight for properly grounded human rights, to help to sing 'these songs of freedom.' But to do that you need to 'emancipate yourselves from mental slavery' of modern ideologies.

> None but ourselves can free our minds
>
> Have no fear for atomic energy
>
> 'Cause none of them can stop the time
>
> How long shall they kill our prophets
>
> While we stand aside and look? Ooh
>
> Some say it's just a part of it
>
> We've got to fullfil the book
>
> Won't you help to sing
>
> These songs of freedom?

GONNA HAVE TO SERVE SOMEBODY

A conversation about religion was postponed until morality could be seen not as rules but for what it truly is – a quality measure of what a free person does. Religions seek to answer the question of the meaning of life, with Christianity pointing out that life's value lies in falling in love with the person of Jesus Christ. Organised religion helps us see the truth of things, keeps sin at bay and provides supernatural help for what is a supernatural journey.

- Over the past few months these regular exchanges have helped clear up much of my woolly thinking. But I must repeat that I am surprised how little you have talked about religion and the afterlife. After all, once a serious discussion about right and wrong starts, ideas of justice and the afterlife cannot be far away. Morality is fundamentally in the zone of religion.

Additionally, the existence of God – and the afterlife – overshadows everything. It seems intensely stupid to me that you would continually ignore it in our discussions. Imagine a party happening in an ordinary suburban garden where an elephant wanders in off the street, and everyone there simply ignores its presence. It would be unthinkable.

- Proper analogies are hard to find, but I would see that garden party being held on a perfectly smooth lawn in well-appointed surroundings, providing a great backdrop to a lively event. In our modern society I see religion serving as that garden: vital to the hosting of a convivial party but ignored and unnoticed by many of the guests. If the lawn and garden surroundings are forever ignored, then the venue will eventually deteriorate to the extent that future parties just won't be possible.

At the heart of all individual and societal challenges lies culture, that is, the way we look at humanity. And at the heart of culture lies questions of meaning and of morality, these being fundamentally religious questions.

Why then have I not talked about religion or the afterlife?

I even imagine you muttering under your breath that I should know better – I am a Christian conscience, after all! I must partially plead guilty to the charge you are making. As Bob Dylan might say, I was a 'Slow Train Coming' on the topic or religion. Rather than 'ignore' the topic, what I have been doing is postponing the discussion. I assure you that I had always intended to get to this point, but I delayed for two good reasons.

First, when these conversations commenced, it was clear from your challenging tone that you did not wish anything imposed on you. So, I wanted you to see your freedom in its true light, that is, as a gift, which if exercised correctly in line with reason could lead you to the truth. Morality is not a question of acceding to diktats nor is it something additional to our nature, superimposed on us by religion. It inheres in our very existence; it is part of who we are. Morality is the measure of what a free person does, and the person finds happiness and fulfilment when they exercise their freedom to achieve what is good and true.

Second, even if you believe you are fully enlightened by the Christian worldview (an understanding that I dispute because you are not sufficiently informed on matters of faith) and did not want me to skirt around religion, I felt a philosophical approach would help prepare you for conversations with your less-religiously committed friends. By my approach I wished to reaffirm that morality is accessible to anyone applying right reason as, quoting St Paul, 'it is written on the human heart'. By using one's reason and one's awareness of human nature, a 'non-religious' person (if such truly exists!) can get a strong handle on the existence of objective right and wrong.

So, I agree with you that we need to talk about religion and how it underpins ideas of freedom. That great freedom fighter, Martin Luther King, once said that 'our lives begin to end when we become silent about the things that matter.'

Freedom is a gift that forms the basis of a person's dignity as a special creation of God. Freedom is fulfilled each time one seeks the true good that is God alone. Your personal experience confirms freedom's inclination to waywardness and error, that it is undermined by personal weakness. Living one's life involves a constant returning to the good path that leads to the final destiny with God.

- Well, if everything is as you say it is, that we can make judgements about right and wrong directly without any further input from God, then why do we need organised religion at all to help us with morality? I can accept that we needed Christ to save us, but once that had been done what more should we need, if everything is written in our hearts?

- Your question has undertones of secularism that need to be addressed first. Once humankind asks about the purpose of life we are in the domain of religion. Secularism tries to shut down discussion by saying that that question is meaningless, arguing this because it doesn't see any way towards answering the question. It often then goes on to explain to you what a meaningful question is: one which can be answered by some empirical measure. Such an answer is woefully inadequate to a society that yearns for some pointers as the purpose of life.

Religions are attempts to answer the question of purpose – and the answers proffered by some religions are woefully inadequate. Christianity on the other hand provides extremely satisfying rational and complete answers although, to the neophyte, the Christian religion, until properly explored, is startling in its most fundamental claims. The Christian response to the question of life's purpose sets freedom in motion in a very specific direction – that of following the person of Jesus Christ.

Religion, in a manner similar to our human nature, stands above culture, looking down on it so to speak, examining it and seeing its flaw and its strengths. As to our need for religion? Organised religion, as you call it, provides a roadmap, with directional aids which point out the pitfalls of the culture more clearly. In that sense it facilitates your freedom.

Without the help of religion, a person can easily become a captive of the culture, as being in tune with that culture does reduce anxiety for the person by insisting that they stay in the safe zone. This is reflected for example in a desire not to stand out, or in a fear of raising one's head above the parapet on a matter of importance to the person. The culture creates an internalised social pressure on the person to engage in actions that he or she may not fully subscribe to. Such actions can be a derogation from the freedom people prize so much. So, when someone argues that they behave in the way they do because 'everyone else is doing it', even though they themselves may not be comfortable with the behaviour, then that person is wasting their freedom. On the other hand, organised religion supports the person to exercise their freedom in the face of cultural pressure.

In 1979, Bob Dylan alienated many of his fans when he came around to singing about religion in his *Slow Train Coming* album. These songs were a mixture of personal faith and religious teaching, stressing some important aspects of Christian morality. His powerful energy and aggressiveness, as expressed in *Gotta Serve Somebody,* reminds us that in exercising freedom we do have to take sides in life.

> But you're gonna have to serve somebody, yes indeed
>
> You're gonna have to serve somebody
>
> Well, it may be the devil or it may be the Lord
>
> But you're gonna have to serve somebody.

Apart from being a measure of your culture, your Christian faith has a lot more to offer than you appreciate. It sets you on a path following the person of Christ. As perfect man he enlightens persons on what is best to do. So, organised religion presents the Gospel message, showing – through life as lived by Christ – what it means to live as an upright moral person.

You can consider following Jesus like falling in love with his person, and consequently loving all those whom he loves. From living one's life like Christ, one begins to see that freedom is founded in love, in giving oneself to others. For a Christian, the other person is never an obstacle to 'my freedom' but is the means through which the Christian is more fully actualised.

- I know I keep nagging you, but can you clear up one point now? Can you personalise this for me? Specifically, I need to know where do I stand in the eyes of God?

- As I said before in response to your query about whether your bad deeds overshadowed your good ones, a question like this is above my pay grade. I can only advise you in the here and now as to the morality of forthcoming actions, admonish you when you don't listen to me, and afterwards review with you anything you have done right or wrong. The answer you are looking for, as to where you stand, lies before the throne of God.

However, it is not as if this should be unfathomable mystery to you, as Christianity provides lots of strong indicators to measure one's relationship with God. To put you at ease I will refresh these for you.

The Christian is called to be a follower of Christ, who is the way, the truth, and the life. In speaking to a rich young man who encounters him and asks him about the requirements of eternal life, Christ indicates that 'If you wish to enter into life, keep the commandments' *(St. Matthew's Gospel 19:17)*. These mandates are all signposts pointing towards love of God. Later, Jesus tells his disciples 'Everyone who has left houses or brothers or sisters or father or mother or children or lands, for my name's sake, will receive a hundredfold and inherit eternal life.' *(St. Matthew 19:29)*. This latter promise would appear to be at the pinnacle of any Christian response. These two Gospel markers provide any person with a lower limit as well as a direction of travel for a relationship with God.

In making a choice to follow Christ, a person is exercising their freedom to seek the truth. On setting out on that path, the person becomes more aware of what is required to keep going. Each step forward on that path is a free step, boosted by the knowledge and assurance that as one approaches what is true and good, one is constantly enhancing one's freedom. The steps are also augmented by God's help, his grace, so that one can continue moving forward. As I said, it's like falling in love, except it is with someone who will never let the loved one down. As a person grows in love, he or she gets to know the truth and to desire it more and more.

People need help to see the path, and to appreciate the value in following it. Yet not everyone will want to follow that path. For example, according to St Pope John Paul II in his encyclical on morality, 'Those who live "by the flesh" experience God's law as a burden, and indeed as a denial or at least a restriction of their own freedom.' (*Veritatis Splendor*, 18).

Help is assured for those who desire it. Apart from the assistance provided by having God's law written on the human heart, the person also has Christ's Church as a guide, as well as that Church providing food for the journey. Christians are alert to their innate tendency to choose self over God and over others, a legacy of original sin. Christians also know that personal sin can easily derail one from the path to God. Thus, the sacraments are vital foodstuffs to get a person to the end, which is eternal happiness with God.

- What you say there about help is very true. My own experience of a sacrament like penance has been limited, but even in psychological terms alone it is a wonderful support. Everyone craves forgiveness, although we can be too proud to seek it. Imagine if God really does forgive sins and that one can begin again, freed of the burden of the past.

- Well, he does forgive! Sin — that is, the rejection of God's will — is what you need to be on the lookout for. Very few people talk about the reality of sin today. Yet there is so much uninvited violence, misfortune and cruelty inflicted on one person by another. Why? Because people have previously succumbed to evil? Because people are carrying burdens of guilt and they lash out at fellow humanity? As you saw with the anger you experienced when you felt that I might be judging you, guilt can be destructive. Truly 'healthy' humans are not those who physically workout daily like you do (fitness is of course important!) but are those who do not suppress truth. By convincing us of the truth of things, God's spirit is not trying to humiliate us, but is seeking to save us from our sin.

  As to where you stand? All persons, whether extremely rich or dirt poor, privileged or oppressed, young or old, are equal before the judgement seat of God — this is the ultimate equality — moral standards are the same for all.

  Can you ever have any certainty as to where you stand? Well, the sacraments seek to make a person worthy to enter God's presence. The answer as to where you stand, not just now but in an ongoing way throughout your life, lies there. It's up to you to use these.

- I like the idea of being a Christian as being akin to someone falling in love. It captures what I would like to achieve in life, and what I would like my friends to achieve as well. Our conversations have clarified how I can advance in this. One thing I need to do going forward is to listen to you more, and not let your voice be drowned out by my appetites and emotions. I suppose you are not called 'the voice of God within' for nothing. But I still have a doubt. How I can I be sure that I will not eventually turn out like the some of my friends, who say they are sincere and authentic in following their conscience, but their behaviour is far from the standard set by Christ? How can I avoid that mistake?

- In the book of Genesis, Adam and Eve's sin was that they wished to be like God. By comparison your culture has gone much further: it is not just satisfied with being like God, it has denied God's very existence. That makes it so much harder for people to do good and avoid evil, as morality disappears from sight when God does. Many Christians today live schizophrenic existences. Outwardly they conform themselves to the expectations of the culture, including all its badness, and inwardly they think themselves to be Christian. They live as if they are in a wartime bunker with no view of the outside world. They consider that all is well because the light and the heat in the bunker are functioning, but they are being fooled by the culture. Their dependence on the greater, outside world is total. To overcome the deception, they need to throw open the windows of their bunker. They need to escape the deceit of secularism and open their eyes to their greatness of the Christian religion.

  You see, once people lose sight of objective truth, their consciences can no longer apply the universal knowledge of the good to their specific behaviour to determine whether their action is right or wrong. What they are doing instead is applying their own standards of good and evil, their 'own truth', and judging their actions by that incomplete or sometimes false standard. In real life no one would want a judge who made up the rules and then adjudicated on his or her own wrongdoing. Yet this is what is happening in the consciences of those people who no longer recognise objective truth.

You want to avoid that mistake, you say. Then remember that the correct exercise of freedom depends on truth. Freedom finds its fulfilment in recognising the truth of who God is and who the human person is. And that truth says that God alone is good. The reality to be acknowledged is that He is at the heart of all. He points out the good to us and helps us achieve it – the latter being subject to the proper use of our freedom.

How can you avoid the mistake of misplacing truth? How can you ensure you see the full truth of things? How can you help your friends to see outside of the bunker? Well, having reasonable and honest discussions like the ones we have had, and not allowing one's passions interfere or claim non-existent rights, can go a long way in helping a person understand where they have gone wrong. Once a person sees the truth, the next step is to really want to respond to it. The truth can be demanding, and as you know yourself, it can be easier not to recognise it so as not to have to follow it.

Returning to the rich young man's encounter with Jesus that I mentioned earlier, Jesus affirms that no one is good but God alone. This is a clear reminder that no one will achieve goodness by one's own efforts. To be truly good, a person needs God's help, his grace, which is available through prayer and sacraments.

- My experience of sin is that it can be like quicksand. Once you are in it then it can be hard to escape from it. Is sin inevitable?

- In our earlier discussions we sought to talk about life in the context of the here and now, while ignoring the afterlife. We focussed on the importance of doing the right thing in the here and now. Implicit in all that discussion was the assumption the right thing in the here-and-now was also objectively right when viewed from the point of view of eternity. Now, I wish to affirm that for any discussion on morality to be complete, it should not ignore the afterlife and eternity. I often think that those with (foolish) utopian ideals are those who have a poor or non-existent sense of the afterlife. They experience within themselves a hope for a better future, but because their horizons are limited to the here and now, they are even ready to ignore the fallibility of human nature in expecting that utopia to be an earthly one.

Your eternal future is a great motivational reality to help you avoid sin, so it should not be ignored. This isn't misusing the promise of heaven. It is using it in the way that is proper to you – you are made for God and for heaven, but it is up to you to exercise your personal freedom to seek him out. Looking to the eternal afterlife gives a fuller meaning to your personal struggle. It is motivational to look forward to the greatness and joys of heaven, and to consider what these might be.

You must not forget that you are human, not an angel, and it is part of your nature to be motivated by a sense of the reward that awaits you. As you grow in love that sense of reward will be displaced by a desire to love God more, but as a fallen human being you should never be ashamed if the consolation of heaven continues to be a motivation.

It becomes apparent when considering the supernatural that you don't have all the tools you need to manage that dimension of your life. In moving beyond the natural something more is needed. Once you desire to live a supernatural life you realise that you need supernatural help. God gives his help or grace to achieve the good, and to avoid the pull of the quicksand. Christ says clearly that God gives his help to those who ask for it. So, the natural is overlaid with the supernatural. To find out more about supernatural life and how to regularly defeat sin in your life will require you to go off and study the tenets of the Christian faith better.

- Now that I see the role for religious faith better, and the need for a relationship with God, I agree that I have more homework to do. I can see that my faith is a truth to be lived out, a path to be followed, and not just theorised about. Apart from you – and I am not belittling your importance nor your efforts in asking this – are there any other supports that I or my friends can rely on?

- Certainly, there is need to go deeper if you wish to be able to explain the reasons for your hope when faced by your modern culture. Don't underestimate the value of the Gospels as a guide.

For those friends who appear not to be ready to entertain any religious reflection, do not be slow to present the added value of Christianity to them and to show how it is a path to happiness.

That primary added value lies in the shortcut that Christianity presents in understanding humankind. God, by becoming man in Jesus Christ, gives us deep insights into humanity itself. Looking to Christ teaches what it means to be fully human: 'Christ reveals man to himself.' When Christ says that no one is good but God alone, he is saying that goodness is a religious question, whose full answer cannot be achieved by mere man-made science. In showing humanity that loving one's neighbour is a prerequisite to loving God, Christ is saying that love is one of the most important signposts to help make sense of existence. Love comes first. Christ shows the full meaning of freedom is to be found in love of God and love of others – shown in service and in self-giving – it is there, among fellow humanity and before God that you fulfil yourself as human.

That Christ would leave humanity with both external and internal supports to guide it in truth makes perfect sense for a loving God who respects personal freedom.

The external way is his Church directed by the Holy Spirit, a guide for individuals and also for the world. Acting like the conscience of the world it is a counterpoint to misplaced secular reason and teaches the world about morality. It also serves as a locus of freedoms.

The internal way to truth is through conscience (that is, me!), that, if properly supported, will align itself to Christ's objective truth. The person and message of Christ provides all men and women with the means of deciphering their lives, in addition to pointing out a clear path to eternal happiness.

So, apart from your human nature telling you what is good and how to exercise your freedom you also have religion. And with religion you have God, you have the person of Christ, you have his signposts – especially his Church, and you have his grace. And you also have me!

What additional support could any person need or want – except, perhaps, a friend like you to remind them of all these available riches? When Bob Dylan really cares about something his message comes across strongly:

> You may be a construction worker working on a home
>
> You may be living in a mansion or you might live in a dome
>
> You might own guns and you might even own tanks
>
> You might be somebody's landlord, you might even own banks
>
> But you're gonna have to serve somebody (serve somebody)
>
> Yes, you're gonna have to serve somebody (serve somebody)
>
> Well, it may be the devil or it may be the Lord
>
> But you're gonna have to serve somebody (serve somebody).

Your care and support for your friends is the best helping hand that they can be given.

STRENGTHEN THE THINGS THAT REMAIN

The acceptance of personal fragility allows one to make room for God and to exercise one's role in the world. The best services a person can provide to culturally confused friends are to present the true value of human nature to them, help them practise charity and ask them to be open in the face of the Christian message. This leads people along a road that replaces fearmongering and lies with trust and truth.

- Now that we have that religious piece well ventilated, I have a suggestion for you. You need to dial back on your neuroticism!

- What? Me? How can you say that? You are the one who designs the guilt trips for me!

- There may be some truth in that, but it is not the full story. Now that you know how everything works – decision making, emotions, reason, conscience, morality – I think you need to establish a greater equanimity and composure. No one is meant to live continually preoccupied by the morality of decisions or a guilt-ridden existence. You see, despite what woke culture utopianism might lead a person to believe, nothing that you do will ever be perfect; it will always have some inadequacies, especially moral ones. There is a danger that you will overlook your human fragility and expect too much from yourself, leading to endless querying about the salvation of your soul. Peace and joy, not anxiety, are the marks of a believer. Imagine someone who makes tiny errors in his job that only he notices, while harbouring thoughts that his next mistake might lead to his dismissal. I don't want you to become like that!

I could appreciate you badgering me a few weeks ago about your eternal soul, but with all the information you have now there is no need for any more neurotic behaviour. Your over-anxious response may have been appropriate due to your past neglect, but now I would like you to try to achieve an even-keel.

- What does that mean in practise? How must my outlook change?

- Being at one with God should not be considered as an additional hurdle that you must cross in this temporal world but should be something inherent in all you do. You should seek to have the enduring intention of behaving like a child of God and then live your life to the full. Or as St Augustine put it, 'love and do what you will!'

This means seeking to see everything with the eyes of eternity, while not backing away from life's many tricky tasks. It requires accepting this world as it is, while working to change it for the good, rather than bemoaning how it might otherwise be and then withdrawing from it. It is to have your head in heaven but simultaneously to have your feet firmly on the ground.

- That advice sounds good to me, but it is not something I can share with others, is it? Many of my colleagues do not have a Christian outlook on life. I am not saying that they are against it, simply they are not aware of what it might mean. How can they operate? How can they do good if God isn't present for them in the world?

-   Some, perhaps the more reflective among them, due to the poor diet provided by woke culture, may be driven by fear or anxiety for the future – they need to be helped to relax! Don't be slow to give that help, to interfere in the lives of your friends and acquaintances. Misplaced personal reserve can be misunderstood as disinterestedness. People want others to show interest in them.

    One piece of advice that you can share with everyone of goodwill is to ask them to be grounded in reality, and to look to human nature, reason and history to point a way forward. That outlook will get them much of the way. If they are genuine in their desire to do good, then there are two further requests you can make of them. First, that they strive to live charity – that is, to put others first – as that helps people to ground themselves socially and to move intellectually beyond the selfishness promoted by individualism. You may also ask them to show a minimum of openness and appreciation of the Christian religious worldview, even if they feel they cannot accede to any of its tenets.

    We have been made to navigate our way successfully through life and to advance our world. While our fallen nature makes that difficult, the proposals above should help open a clear path for your friends.

-   You may be surprised to hear me say this, but I fully agree with your assessment of me. I was showing signs of neuroticism over the past few weeks. Now that I have a better understanding of the lie of the land, I think I am more relaxed and better prepared to solve the problems of this world.

- You are staking a claim in a major undertaking there – to solve the problems of the world! And might I ask, how do you propose doing that? What will your guiding principles be? Bob Dylan, one of the early voices of the freedom movement, was a surprise choice as a Nobel Literature prizewinner for his meaningful lyrics. In his *Slow Train Coming* album he displayed a real intolerance with fellow Christians about the state of the world and continually chided them in *When You Gonna Wake Up* for tolerating its badness. In a series of verses, he complains about many of the evils in politics, justice, medicine and business. Between each verse he demands a personal response from the listener:

  When you gonna wake up, when you gonna wake up

  When you gonna wake up strengthen the things that remain?

  What exactly is your approach going to be to the world that you wish to change? I am not sure Dylan's anger and seeming intolerance went down well with his listeners.

- His message has solid content despite what us moderns might consider as his harsh language. These days, no matter how true it might be, you cannot say to people,

  (You got) adulterers in churches and pornography in the schools

  You got gangsters in power and lawbreakers making rules.

  When you gonna wake up, when you gonna wake up

  When you gonna wake up strengthen the things that remain?

I prefer the methodology you mapped out earlier as the best way to approach people of goodwill. It is clear from our discussions that traditional secular liberalism cannot rescue our society. In presenting the enlightened scientific world-view as the only route available to humanity it has denied our experience of reality, our human nature and the enduring necessity of human interdependence. This liberalism has now undergone its own scientific evolution into wokeness – a necessary progression as cold individualism had little sustaining power – and there is no going back. Christian ideals slowed liberalism's evolution into secularism for the past two centuries, but such resistance has gradually lost its public potency in the Western world. Liberal global capitalism's opportunistic decision to cloak itself in woke thinking may eventually backfire on capitalism as increasing wealth disparities continue along unsustainable paths. Alternatively, it is conceivable that woke capitalism may find itself out-flanked by hard-core capitalist thinking that does not allow sentiment to interfere with profit. But for now, wokeism rules the roost. So, your approaches of encouraging people to be grounded in the reality of their human nature, promoting the practise of charitable deeds and asking people to be open to exploring the Christian worldview seem to the best route to maintaining the freedoms we so obviously need.

Additionally, I have been thinking about what can be learned from our current world crises – particularly the pandemic and global warming – and humankind's responses. Evident mistakes can often be good pointers to more worthwhile future alternative solutions.

Covid-19 scared most of us into the hands of vaccine manufacturers. The reasonable and, subsequently, mostly justified claims of big pharma helped reassure and protect many lives. Yet some inexplicable omissions by officialdom caused other people to stay clear of the vaccine offerings. Why not tell us about alternative effective treatments? Why hide negative data on the vaccines? Why not be open with one's citizens? The unsurprising, non-universal acceptance of vaccine mandates provided further fuel for siren calls that in turn reinforced others in their suspicions. These issues, combined with historic popular distrust of governments – especially in former communist countries – impeded vaccine take-up. Just as attempts at compulsion in some countries led to a lower uptake of the vaccines, so too did the reduced transparency on Covid-origins and on vaccine deficiencies drive a distrust in governmental intentions. One wonders what might have happened if citizens had witnessed and experienced a greater openness and allegiance to truth.

Further learning can be had from considering responses to the global warming threat. Climate change activists want the planet saved, yet how can that be achieved? They present the science to us, yet many people – although the number diminishes as each climate prophecy is presented as having been fulfilled – remain sceptical. They tell us that it's our children who will suffer most. That argument lacks compulsion when they also recommend to us that we should not have any children. But the science continues to be highly uncertain – with natural sceptics easily reading between the lines.

So, climate warriors have chosen to frighten us, to alarm us, to add further to our generation's emotional fragility. Every major weather event becomes proof of the emergency. That seems to work, in that it causes our elected leaders to make unreal or unrealisable promises. And on it goes – fright, followed by inadequate reaction, and then frighten further. But who really believes that targeted carbon reductions are achievable through this re-affirmation of fear? When these methods are seen not to work, will 'they' then feel compelled to employ more authoritarian tactics?

My solution lies not in the methods of cover-up – as with Covid – nor of fear – as with climate change. It sits, as we have spoken of before, with truth. So out with lies and fearmongering. Let reality be our guide, tell the truth!

- I share your identification of the lie as our real enemy, but it interesting that you should also focus in on fearmongering. The British author, CS Lewis, in *The Screwtape Letters* highlights the need for courage in life. He saw that for people to be good required courage. Lewis was concerned that continually presenting small unconscious reservations and fears to people's minds would slowly make cowards of everyone. The greater the fear-mongering the more cowards that are created. It then may be the case that the drip drip effect of climate anxiety and of pandemic fears is undermining the courage of this generation.

- Yes, it is easy to end up living a very precautionary life in today's world, feeling threatened by even words themselves, seeing these as violence, as we identified earlier with woke culture.

When it comes to truth telling, courage is what is required, not cowardice. We need more truth telling. People trust those who tell the truth – we respond best when the truth is told to us. We all can gather around the truth. It may not be easily attainable, we may not always agree on what it is, but insofar as we are seen to be striving for it, we will learn to trust each other. When we see honesty, we recognise it.

Honest gatekeepers of knowledge are distinguishable from fake fact-checkers in a society that places a store on truth. Honesty is persuasive in more ways that deceit could ever be.

- I admire your trust in humanity. I have always felt you were more understanding of others than I might be. But I dare to suggest now that you are naïve. Misinformation and lies have always been with us. These are not new realities. By exposing us to more information perhaps social media has also exposed us to more lies. The situation has been aggravated in democratic societies by a lack of allegiance to truth-telling principles by the corporate media.

- Yes, but you also affirmed before that 'the truth will set us free'. So that is where we must begin… and begin again. Tell the truth, build up trust, stand up for truth. Then we can have real worthwhile communication.

I am not as naïve as this appeal might make me sound. I heartily realise that our institutions and our elites are not going to rescue us – for the most part these are no longer anchored in reality. Your presentation earlier of Winston Marshall's stand, his very own 'personal non-participation in lies', is to be my way forward too.

- Are you not concerned that you are sounding somewhat religious now – that such moral insistence might not go down well in your secular society? Do you not think that in fact you are shooting yourself in the foot at a time when you are also seeking to grow common ground in resolving the world's problems?

- Our current difficulties are due to secularism. It has removed objectivity from our world – it has undermined man's search for truth. The so-called death of God is old news, and we are now well positioned to fully examine the sad impact of that claim. In turning away from God, we turned away from the truths we need in order to fully understand ourselves, leading us to become pawns of materialist ideologies. In facing up to truth there is likely to be secular resistance – this a reality I am ready to face.

In any event, it is the Christian religious worldview that has the deepest interest in saving our world. For it, the world needs to be redeemed, as it is to form a basis for the eternal world to come. 'Isms' will come and go but today it is Christians who will do their best for this world because in doing so they see themselves shaping the eternal tomorrow.

All the principles of freedom we have talked about – respect for life, for liberty and for others, are interconnected. When one principle is abandoned the rest fall away, one by one. A society that doesn't respect the human life of another person will come to disrespect all other freedoms, one after another. That is the situation our Western society finds itself in, and secularism's only solution, as evidenced in wokeism, is the further oppression of disparate voices. Humanity's future lies in the defence of truth, in seeing the good as good, or as Dylan seems to be saying 'in strengthen(ing) the things that remain.' As to who all those defenders of that truth will be we cannot presume, but I for one can at least put my shoulder to the wheel.

- Well, count on me to be there with you. Having achieved such alignment over these past months I have no doubt we will make a great team!

Appendix

LIVE NOT BY LIES

The famous Russia dissident author Aleksandr Solzhenitsyn was arrested in Russia in 1974. This prompted him to immediately publish the text of what has become his most famous essay, *Live Not by Lies*. The then communist USSR regime subsequently exiled Solzhenitsyn to Western Europe, where as the author of the *Gulag Archipelago* and a prominent communist dissident, he was received as a hero. For Solzhenitsyn, 'lies' equated with ideology, the illusion that human nature and society can be reshaped in line with some predetermined plan. In his *Live Not By Lies* essay – which provided inspiration for the last chapter in this book – Solzhenitsyn highlights some specific ways in which one can avoid 'personal participation in the lie'.

The term dissident has now reappeared in the West to identify those who are reluctant to accept what is seen as a Western elitist worldview, infused with woke thinking. Included in this group are those who questioned some of the Covid pandemic responses, those opposed to vaccine mandates such as Canada's 2022 Freedom Convoy, opponents of gender ideology and those who question the wisdom of big tech exercising censorship powers. The term has gradually been extended to include broadcasters such America's top podcaster, Joe Rogan, who insists that alternative viewpoints should receive a public hearing and to some public intellectuals quoted in this book. The method of the modern dissident continues to be that which was successfully deployed by Solzhenitsyn – the pointing to the facts, the call for evidence, the revelation of truth.

To better inform the reader we quote from Solzhenitsyn's essay here, which is best understood if considered as a gentle, personal plea to all:

> And thus, overcoming our temerity, let each man choose: Will he remain a witting servant of the lies (needless to say, not due to natural predisposition, but in order to provide a living for the family, to rear the children in the spirit of lies!), or has the time come for him to stand straight as an honest man, worthy of the respect of his children and contemporaries? And from that day onward he:
>
> - Will not write, sign, nor publish in any way, a single line distorting, so far as he can see, the truth.
> - Will not utter such a line in private or in public conversation, nor read it from a crib sheet, nor speak it in the role of educator, canvasser, teacher, actor.
> - Will not in painting, sculpture, photograph, technology, or music depict, support, or broadcast a single false thought, a single distortion of the truth as he discerns it.
> - Will not cite in writing or in speech a single "guiding" quote for gratification, insurance, for his success at work, unless he fully shares the cited thought and believes that it fits the context precisely.
> - Will not be forced to a demonstration or a rally if it runs counter to his desire and his will; will not take up and raise a banner or slogan in which he does not fully believe.

- Will not raise a hand in vote for a proposal which he does not sincerely support; will not vote openly or in secret ballot for a candidate whom he deems dubious or unworthy.
- Will not be impelled to a meeting where a forced and distorted discussion is expected to take place.
- Will at once walk out from a session, meeting, lecture, play, or film as soon as he hears the speaker utter a lie, ideological drivel, or shameless propaganda.
- Will not subscribe to, nor buy in retail, a newspaper or journal that distorts or hides the underlying facts.

This is by no means an exhaustive list of the possible and necessary ways of evading lies. But he who begins to cleanse himself will, with a cleansed eye, easily discern yet other op- portunities....

(© 2006 English-language copyright Yermolai Solzhenitsyn)

REFERENCES

Chapter 1
Chapter title and quotes from *The Sound of Silence*. Originally *The Sounds of Silence*, released on Simon and Garfunkel debut album *Wednesday Morning, 3 A.M. The Sound of Silence* lyrics © Paul Simon Music. The chapter additionally includes quotes from *Human* by The Killers. *Human* lyrics © Universal Music Publishing Ltd.

Chapter 2
Chapter title and quotes from *Shallow* (from *A Star is Born* film). *Shallow* lyrics © Sony/atv Songs Llc, Downtown Dmp Songs, Downtown Dlj Songs, Songs Of Zelig, White Bull Music Group, Stephaniesays Music, Warner Olive Music Llc., Warner-barham Music Llc., Concord Copyrights, Sg Songs Worldwide.

Chapter 3
Chapter title and quotes from *This Land Is Your Land* by Woodie Guthrie. Aleksandr Solzhenitsyn quotes from *The Gulag Archipelago 1918–1956* by Aleksandr Solzhenitsyn, (1973, Harper Collins).

Chapter 4
Chapter title and quotes from *Turn, Turn, Turn* © songwriter Peter Seeger. Additional quotes from *The Times They Are A-Changin*. Songwriter: Bob Dylan. *The Times They Are A-Changin'*

lyrics © Sony/ATV Music Publishing LLC and from *Blowing In The Wind*. Songwriters: Bob Dylan. *Blowin` In The Wind* lyrics © Special Rider Music, Universal Tunes.

Chapter 5
Chapter title and quotes from *The Island* by Paul Brady. Songwriters: Geoffrey Downes / Trevor Charles Horn. *The Island* lyrics © Universal Music Publishing Group.

Chapter 6
Chapter title and quotes from *The Cave* by Mumford and Sons. Songwriters: Benjamin Walter David Lovett / Edward James Milton Dwane / Marcus Oliver Johnstone Mumford / Winston Aubrey Aladar Marshall. *The Cave* lyrics © Universal Music Publishing Group.
Bret Weinstein (and Heather Heying) are evolutionary biologists whose uncomfortable scientific speculations have persistently challenged big tech suppression (see for example *DarkHorse* podcasts on YouTube). In his podcasts Bret uses the term martyr (see Chapter 5) to describe the brave actions of some scientists.

Chapter 7
Chapter title and quotes from *Human* by The Killers. Songwriters: Vannucci Ronnie / Keuning Dave Brent / Flowers Brandon / Stoermer Mark August.

Human lyrics © Universal Music Publishing Ltd. The William Shakespeare quote is from *Hamlet*, Act 2 Scene 2.

Chapter 8
Chapter title and quotes from *If I Didn't Have Your Love* by Leonard Cohen. Songwriters: Leonard Cohen / Patrick Leonard. *If I Didn't Have Your Love* lyrics © Universal Music Corp., Old Ideas Llc, No Tomato Music, Pw Arrangements.
Additional quotes from *Do They Know It's Christmas?* by Band Aid (1984). Songwriters: Midge Ure / Bob Geldof. *Do They Know It's Christmas?* lyrics © Chappell Music Lt.

Chapter 9
Chapter title and quotes from *Ramblin' Man* by Hank Williams. Songwriter: Shelton Hank III Williams. *Ramblin' Man* Lyrics © Sony/ATV Music Publishing Llc, Mike Curb Music.

Chapter 10
Chapter title and quotes from *Lost Cause* by Billy Eilish. Songwriters: Billie Eilish O'Connell / Finneas Baird O'Connell. *Lost Cause* lyrics © Universal Music Corp., Last Frontier, Drup. Biography reference is to Bob Geldof's biography *Is that it?* (Pan Macmillan 1986).

Chapter 11
Chapter title and quotes from *Strange Fruit* by Billy Holiday. Songwriter: Lewis Allan. *Strange Fruit* lyrics © Wb Music Corp., Music Sales Corporation, Edward B Marks Music Company, Marks Edward B. Music Corp., Edward B. Marks Music Co., Dwayne Wiggins Pub Designee.
Elie Wiesel quote is from his lecture *The Perils of Indifference* (The White House, Washington. 1999)
St Augustine quote is from his *In Iohannis Evangelium Tractatus*, 41, 10.

Chapter 12
Chapter title and quotes from *I'm Not Anyone* by Paul Anka. Songwriters: Johnny Harris / Paul Anka. *I'm Not Anyone* lyrics © BMG Rights Management US, LLC.
Additional quotes from *All of Me* by John Legend. Songwriters: John Stephens / Toby Gad. *All of Me* lyrics © John Legend Publishing, Gad Songs, Atlas Music Publishing Llc.

Chapter 13
Chapter title and quotes from *On Raglan Road* a poem/song by Patrick Kavanagh.
Quote about 'the line dividing between good and evil' is from *The Gulag Archipelago 1918–1956* by Aleksandr Solzhenitsyn (1973 Harper Collins). For Jordan Peterson on evil see *Maps of Meaning* (2000 Taylor & Francis, Routledge).Wi
lliam Shakespeare quote is from *Richard III* Act 5, scene 3.
Zerocalcare is the Italian comic-strip artist Michele Rech, creator of *Tear Along the Dotted Line* (Netflix).

Chapter 14

Chapter title and quotes from *The Fields of Athenry* by songwriter Pete St John (1979).

Additional quotes from *Me and Bobby McGee* by Kris Kristofferson. Songwriters: F. Foster / K. Kristofferson. *Me and Bobby McGee* lyrics © Combine Music Corp.

Dorothy Day quote is from *What Catholics don't understand about communism* in America Magazine April 19, 1933.

Oscar Wilde quote is from *The Soul of Man Under Socialism* (first published March 15, 1891). Available from Kessinger Publishing (2004).

John Stuart Mill quote is from *Inaugural Address Delivered to the University of St Andrews, 2/1/1867*. Available in *Collected Works of John Stuart Mill* (Classic Books, 2000).

Chapter 15

Chapter title and quotes from *Fairy Tale of New York* by The Pogues. Songwriters: Jem Finer / Shane Patrick Lysaght Macgowan. *Fairytale of New York* lyrics © Sony/ATV Music Publishing LLC, Universal Music Publishing Group.

Chapter 16

Chapter title and quotes from *You Have Loved Enough* from Leonard Cohen album, *Ten New Songs*. Songwriters: Cohen Leonard / Robinson Sharon. *You Have Loved Enough* lyrics © Emi April Music Inc., Sony/atv Songs Llc.

Chapter 17

Chapter title and quotes from *Redemption Song* by Bob Marley. Songwriter: John Ashton Thomas. *Redemption Song* lyrics © Odnil Music Ltd., Fifty Six Hope Road Music Ltd., Blackwell Fuller Music Publishing Llc.

Chapter 18

Chapter title and quotes from *Gotta Serve Somebody* in *Slow Train Coming* album, Bob Dylan, 1979. Songwriter: Bob Dylan. *Gotta Serve Somebody* lyrics © Sony/ATV Music Publishing LLC.

Martin Luther King (1965) quote is from *I Have a Dream: Writings and Speeches That 'Changed the World* by Martin Luther King Jr., James Melvin Washington (Editor) HarperOne (1987)

Quote from *Veritatis Splendor* encyclical is from Section 18, by St Pope John Paul II.

'Christ reveals man' quote from *Gaudium et Spes*, Vatican II (1965).

Chapter 19

Chapter title and quotes from *When You Gonna Wake Up?* (Slow Train Coming album by Bob Dylan). Songwriter: Bob Dylan. *When You Gonna Wake Up?* lyrics © Sony/ATV Music Publishing LLC.

THEMATIC INDEX